SECOND EDIT[...]

MW01012417

Practically Painless English

SALLY FOSTER WALLACE
Parkland College

PRENTICE HALL Upper Saddle River, NJ 07458

Library of Congress Cataloging-in-Publication Data

Wallace, Sally Foster
    Practically painless English / Sally Foster Wallace. -- 2nd ed.
        p.   cm.
    Includes bibliographical references.
    ISBN 0-13-692781-5 :
    1. English language--Rhetoric. 2. English language-
  -Grammar--1950-   I. Title.
    PE1408.W31322 1989
    428.2--dc20   89-36295
                                                          CIP

Editorial/production supervision and
  interior design: Arthur Maisel
Cover design: Wanda Lubelska
Manufacturing buyer: Ray Keating

© 1990, 1980 by Prentice-Hall, Inc.
A Pearson Education Company
Upper Saddle River, NJ 07458

Printed in the United States of America
10 9 8 7 6 5 4

ISBN 0-13-692781-5

Prentice-Hall International (UK) Limited,London
Prentice-Hall of Australia Pty. Limited, Sydney
Prentice-Hall Canada Inc., Toronto
Prentice-Hall Hispanoamericana, S.A., Mexico
Prentice-Hall of India Private Limited, New Delhi
Prentice-Hall of Japan, Inc., Tokyo
Pearson Education Asia Pte. Ltd., Singapore
Editora Prentice-Hall do Brasil, Ltda., Rio de Janeiro

for my brother, Fenton Gerald Foster, and for Liz, his joy

Contents

8   *Bits of Fascination*   *139*

Preface

This is the second edition of *Practically Painless English* and, like the first one, it strives to convey the fun and excitement of learning the essentials of English grammar and composition. Although the book takes a light-hearted, user-friendly approach, it is still a serious attempt to involve students in the practically painless pizzazz and joy of English and to help them view writing as a way of learning about themselves and their world.

Those already familiar with *PPE* will notice some new characters: Peony McAllister ventures forth on her motorcycle, cheered on by Rambo and Rambette, Inertia and Aphasia, Grandma and Grandpa Pringle, and Chively Sneed. Among the old characters, Fedonia Krump appears to have mellowed somewhat, but Mongo hasn't changed a bit.

This new and improved handbook/workbook reflects several suggestions from students, colleagues, and far-flung correspondents: all of the material in the exercises and in the cumulative tests and in most of the examples is new; the answers to all the answerable exercises appear in the back of the book; there is a glossary of terms and a punctuation-rules-at-a-glance section for quick reference; there are a few words about figurative language; and there are 160 paragraph-writing topics and more than 100 topics for longer compositions. The explanations of restrictive and nonrestrictive elements, of various kinds of clauses, and of pronoun agreement have been expanded, and *anxious/eager, farther/further,* and *nauseated/nauseous* are added to the section about using words correctly.

I thank Phil Miller, Prentice Hall Humanities Editor, for his good-humored patience and encouragement; James D. Wallace for lessons on the Macintosh Plus and for help of all kinds at all times; David F. and Amy E. Wallace, who are constant sources of joy and inspiration; Sharon Butts and Chauncy Cranston Irvine for friendship of the purest ray serene; and John Robert Glasa, proofreader extraordinaire. My gratitude to my students knows no bounds.

Sally Foster Wallace

SECTION 1 *Parts of Speech*

Knowing the parts of speech will not magically make you a good, clear, effective writer; some people who can't tell an adjective from an elephant write beautifully. Such writers have usually been surrounded by precise English all their lives, and they also seem to enjoy reading anything they can get their eyes on.

Many people, though, need help to understand what kinds of words can be put together to express an idea precisely, and this is a reason for learning the old-fashioned parts of speech. If the inner workings of English have always seemed mysterious to you, knowing the parts of speech will help you solve the mystery and understand what a logical, beautiful, organized language English is. Once you know the parts of speech, you can discuss the language intelligently; you can refer to an adverb or a preposition, just as an architect can refer to a buttress or an arch.

Also, knowing the parts of speech in English is valuable if you decide to study another language. Your German, French, Spanish, Russian, or Swahili teachers will refer constantly to pronouns, verbs, nouns, conjunctions, and other classifications of words; if you know their English counterparts, you'll find learning the second language easier.

Knowing the parts of speech can help you develop your writing skills; you can recognize and reorganize groups of words that lack important parts or that have parts in the wrong places or in the wrong forms. As you become more and more

1

interested in English, you'll be glad that you know the parts of speech. This section will introduce you to each of the eight parts of speech, give you exercises, and end with a small test to let you know how much you have learned.

NOUNS

A **common noun** names a person, place, thing, relationship, concept, or idea.

Eight-toed **wombats** need **love,** too.
In just one **week,** my **car** lost its **wheels, hood,** and **bumper.**
When you go to the **store,** please get some **garters** for my **snake.**
Our **nation** believes in **life, liberty,** and the **pursuit** of **happiness.**

Exercise

Please circle the common nouns in this list of words:

little	feebly
ant	witch
cabbage	hill
crawled	geranium
beauty	over
cousin	sharpen
wonderful	eraser
slowly	erase

A **proper noun** is the name of a specific person, place, thing, language, country, day, month, or religion.

Proper nouns are always capitalized. (The first word of a sentence is always capitalized, too, so don't automatically assume that the first word of a sentence is a proper noun.)

Peony McAllister sings songs in **Spanish** at the **Heartbreak Hotel** every **Tuesday.**
The water stain on my ceiling is in the shape of **Australia.**
Nuthatch, my pet squirrel, loves to dance to the music of **Tchaikovsky.**
Mongo Munyon plans to roller-skate to **Maine, Michigan, Montana,** and **Mississippi** in **May.**

Exercise

Please circle the proper nouns in the following sentences:

1. Large bats visit Bear Paw Pond on the third Tuesday of each October.
2. Dr. Seuss used to live on Mulberry Street in Christmas Cove, New Hampshire.

3. Rambo Hutchinson drinks Diet Coke and eats nails.

4. Mr. Smith went to Washington, but he was homesick for Kalamazoo.

Exercise

In the following sentences, circle each common noun that you find and capitalize each proper noun:

1. Fedonia krump is a little old lady from pasadena, so she needs tea and sympathy.

2. Mrs. johnson called her twin boys pete and repeat.

3. I'd like to visit dallas, so I could tell j. r. ewing to shape up.

4. The easter bunny put all his eggs in one basket, so when he tripped over mike's bicycle, the yolk was on him.

5. Venus flytrap is one of grandma's favorite characters on television.

6. When eric studies french, he eats only toast and fries.

7. Dad's corn crop should be neck high by the end of july.

8. Do you think fred and wilma will let pebbles become a rock star?

9. On mondays and wednesdays, the parking lot is full of toyotas, hondas, and fords.

10. After the dallas cowpeople win the superbowl, they'll have a rodeo in madison square garden in new york city.

Exercise

From your own storehouse of words, list five common nouns:

1. _____

2. _____

3. _____

4. _____

5. _____

Now list five proper nouns:

1. _____

2. _____

3. _____

4. _____

5. _____

PRONOUNS

A **pronoun** is a word that can take the place of a noun.

Pronouns are very handy; if we didn't have them, we would have to repeat nouns all the time, and our speech and writing would be bulky and boring.

He has two attack-trained roosters, and **I**'m afraid of **them**.
You and **I** should burn **our** VCR, so **we** can get some studying done.
If **he** makes **his** wounded-rhinoceros noise again, **I**'ll scream.
Little Bo Peep has lost **her** eight-toed wombats, and **she** doesn't know where to find **them**.
His goldfish is shinier than **yours**.

Here are some popular pronouns that you probably use every day:

I	them	ours	yourself
you	my	who	himself
he	mine	whose	herself
she	your	whom	itself
it	yours	everyone	ourselves
we	his	someone	yourselves
they	hers	no one	themselves
me	its	everybody	this
him	their	somebody	that
her	theirs	nobody	these
us	our	myself	those

Don't be terrified by this list; it merely shows you that some of your most useful words are pronouns. For more fascinating facts about pronouns, see Section 6.

Remember that *I* is the only pronoun that is always capitalized, no matter where it appears in a sentence. Capitalize a pronoun referring to God, too:

God's eye is on the sparrow, but I know He watches me.

Exercise

Replace the *italicized* words with appropriate pronouns.

1. Mongo and Fedonia hoped to visit the Bubblegum Museum, but *the Bubblegum Museum* exploded before *Mongo and Fedonia* got there.
2. Lizzo is allergic to yogurt, granola, and tofu, so *Lizzo* makes sure to pick *yogurt, granola, and tofu* out of *Lizzo's* pizza.
3. Chively Sneed told *Chively Sneed's* aunt that *Chively Sneed's aunt's* henhouse was on fire; *Chively Sneed's aunt* told *Chively Sneed* that *Chively Sneed* could have fried chicken for *Chively Sneed's* dinner.
4. Aphasia McGurk likes Larry, Curly, and Mo, but *Aphasia McGurk* doesn't plan to name *Aphasia McGurk's* new triplets after *Larry, Curly, and Mo*.

5. If Ethelred's favorite song is "I'll Be Down to Get You in a Taxi, Honey," why doesn't *Ethelred* ever play *"I'll Be Down to Get You in a Taxi, Honey"* on *Ethelred's* electronic kazoo?

Exercise

Please circle each pronoun you find in these sentences:

1. When you grow too old to dream, you'll have us to remember.
2. He declared war on the woodchucks in his garden, so they moved to yours.
3. Al and Ben planted catnip in their mailbox.
4. Joan and Jane took their pet eight-toed wombat camping with them, and it ate their tent.
5. Fedonia saves her used teabags and wears them as earrings.
6. George loves squid sherbet, so Martha makes it for him every day.
7. If you don't clean your room today, Mongo, I'm going to ask the Health Department to condemn it.
8. I took one look at the monster's jaws, and my heart jumped out of my chest.
9. They refused to pay their power bill, so they're dancing in the dark.
10. Lassie is teaching her pups to chew with their mouths open.

VERBS

A **verb** indicates action or state of being.

Time **waits** for no one, but the other magazines **are** quite patient.
Chively Sneed now **hates** fried chicken.
The chef **whipped** the cream, **scrambled** the eggs, and **diced** his apron.
Mongo **is** my sunshine.

Note of caution: don't think that a verb is always just one word—look at this:

That road **should have been opened** to traffic last week, but the bulldozer **has been stuck** in the mud for three weeks.
The Great Pumpkin **will give** me a Halloween present.

(Section 7 will tell you all you ever wanted to know about verbs.)

Exercise

Please supply your own verbs to complete the following sentences:

1. When the moon comes over the mountain, it _____ .
2. Rocky and Maybelline like to exercise, so they _____ ,
    _____ , and _____ every morning.

3. If it doesn't rain tomorrow, will you _____ ?

4. The eight-toed wombat _____ when it's hungry.

5. My cousin once _____ a kangaroo.

6. Chively Sneed _____ once a week.

7. When you _____ too much, you always _____ .

8. He _____ the goat, so it _____ him.

9. Clorene _____ toucans, but she _____ sharks.

10. The ghost _____ and _____ , but I

_____ .

Exercise

Please circle each verb you find in these sentences:

1. The mice complained when the cat dynamited their house.
2. When you go to the store, please buy some bees' knees for dessert.
3. Amy and Heather drove to Charlottesville and lost their way only twice.
4. Rambo opened his eyes, rose from his barbed-wire bed, and bathed with gasoline and a wire brush.
5. The prince danced with Snow White, and Grumpy was jealous.

ADJECTIVES

An **adjective** describes a noun or a pronoun.

I plan to wear a **funny** hat, a **torn** shirt, and **plaid** shoes to our **peculiar** neighbor's **weekly** party.
Whistling girls and **crowing** hens will always come to **some strange** end, according to the **weird old** fortuneteller.
Eighteen tiny, dancing, purple-nosed elves live in the **tall, sticky** tree.
Uncle Abner got an **interesting** letter from the **local** branch of Tax Collectors **Anonymous.**

Adjectives that are formed from proper nouns are known as **proper adjectives,** and they are always capitalized.

I am allergic to **French** poodles, **Arabian** horses, and **Russian** wolfhounds.

Exercise

Please circle the adjectives in the following paragraph:

It was a dark and stormy night, but brave, beautiful Peony McAllister quickly finished her dinner of Swedish meatballs, Russian tea, English muffins, and Norwegian sardines, put on her fuchsia boots, grabbed her frilly umbrella, and made her lonely way through the inky alley. Terrified, she bumped into a huge, water-soaked box, fell over an abandoned skateboard, and leaped over a muddy puddle. Her nervous laughter echoed through the half-empty garage, but her bright brown eyes finally found the object of her frantic search, and, as she kick-started her trusty motorcycle, she gave a loud cheer, glad that she wouldn't be late for her nightly Japanese flower-arranging class.

ARTICLES

Technically, *a*, *an*, and *the* are adjectives, but they are usually referred to as **articles.**

The **is a definite article:** "*the* tree" specifies a particular tree, and your reader or listener awaits more information about it:

The tree in **the** front yard has turned purple.
The apple on **the** table contains half a worm.

A and *an* are **indefinite articles:** "*a* tree" doesn't specify a particular tree; "*an* apple" doesn't specify a particular apple.

Use *an* before a word that begins with a vowel sound:

an apple	an ape	
an elf	an ear	
an irregularity	an island	an eye
an occurrence	an oaf	

an hour (the *h* is silent, so the first sound you hear is the *o*)
an uncle (words beginning with *u* are particularly tricky; if the *u* is short, as in *uncle* or *underwear*, you need *an*; if the *u* is long, as in *united* or *universe*, you need merely *a*)

Exercise

In the following sentences, supply *a* or *an*:

1. Mongo said that he saw _____ unicorn yesterday.

2. I'm in the mood for _____ ham and jam sandwich.

3. If there's _____ anchovy on this pizza, Clorene won't touch it.

4. _____ sheriff, _____ bailiff, and _____ mastiff are arriving on _____ airplane this afternoon.

5. _____ pirate wearing _____ eyepatch stole my favorite snake.

6. The principal noticed _____ alarming irregularity in Smedley's attendance.

7. I'd settle for _____ B, but Miss Piggy is desperate for _____ A in our swine management course.

8. When I offered Chively Sneed _____ fried-chicken dinner, he made _____ abrupt exit.

9. When the circus train jumped the tracks, _____ elephant, _____ eland, _____zebra, and _____ eight-toed wombat escaped.

10. The recipe for Witch's Surprise calls for _____ owl's ear and _____ bee's eyebrow.

11. I've heard that half _____ loaf is better than none, so I took _____ half-day off from work.

12. On Saturdays, _____ aisle in _____ grocery store seems like _____ active anthill.

13. Let _____ smile be your umbrella, and you'll end up with _____ awful cold.

14. _____ elm tree is a rare sight in the Midwest, but there seems to be _____ locust tree on every corner.

15. My new diet lets me have _____ ice-cream cone _____ hour.

ADVERBS

Adverbs describe verbs, adjectives, and other adverbs.

Rambo giggled **nervously.** (*Nervously* describes the verb *giggled.*)
When Elmo had laryngitis, he was **quite** quiet. (*Quite* describes the adjective *quiet.*)
Mongo bought that fuchsia house **rather** hastily, didn't he? (*Rather* describes the adverb *hastily.*)
You're **too** nice to be forgotten. (*Too* describes the adjective *nice.*)
The **bright** orange flag has holes in it. (*Bright* describes the adjective *orange.*)

Many adverbs end in *ly* (*swiftly, slowly, gracefully, beautifully*), but some don't (*fast, much, well, rather, too, very*), so the ending isn't a surefire way to identify an adverb. The best way to recognize an adverb is to ask yourself if that word describes a verb, an adjective, or an adverb. If so, the word is an adverb.

Also, it is helpful to remember that adverbs usually answer such questions as *when, where, how,* or *to what extent.*

We'll be moving to Tasmania **soon.** (*when*)
Sit **right here,** young man, and don't move a muscle! (*where*)
Kermit **truly** admires Miss Piggy. (*how*)
I'm **extremely** nervous about swimming in the shark tank. (*to what extent*)

Exercise

Please supply your own adverbs in the following sentences:

1. Alvin tackles _____ , but he passes _____ .
2. I dislike anchovies _____ , so I avoid them
   _____ .
3. Aunt Hagatha has a _____ bald canary.
4. If you don't swim _____ , Jason will catch you!
5. Fedonia has _____ few teeth to win the flossing award.

Exercise

Please circle the adverbs in the following paragraph:

   Peony McAllister was so excited about her extremely interesting Japanese flower-arranging class that she completely ignored the bright red stop signs randomly placed here and there on her route to school. Suddenly, her very cold ears picked up the hauntingly familiar sound of a skull-shatteringly loud siren, and she saw dazzling lights in her rearview mirror. Frantically, she began to create convincingly pathetic excuses for going too fast. As she slowly pulled over to the side of the road, she patted her motorcycle tenderly and smiled bravely at the very large person who was slowly approaching.

PREPOSITIONS

A **preposition** shows the relation of a noun or pronoun to some other word in the sentence. In the examples, notice how the preposition changes the runner's location in relation to the gorilla.

I am running **with** the gorilla.
I am running **for** the gorilla.
I am running **to** the gorilla.
I am running **beside** the gorilla.
I am running **behind** the gorilla.
I am running **from** the gorilla.
I am running **over** the gorilla.
I am running **under** the gorilla.
I am running **around** the gorilla.
I am running **across** the gorilla.
I am running **on** the gorilla.
I am running **through** the gorilla.

A group of words that begins with a preposition and ends with a noun or pronoun is called a **prepositional phrase:** *with the gorilla, for the gorilla, to the gorilla,* etc.

The following words are commonly used as prepositions:

abroad	at	by
about	before	concerning
above	behind	down
across	below	during
after	beneath	for
against	beside	from
along	between	in
among	beyond	into
around	through	until
off	to	with
on	toward	without
since	under	like

Some prepositions consist of more than one word: *in spite of* my warning, *on account of* the flood, *according to* Freud.

Exercise

Please use each of the following prepositions in a sentence:

1. without _____

2. beyond _____

3. against _____

4. until _____

5. from _____

CONJUNCTIONS

A **conjunction** joins words, phrases, clauses, or sentences.

Gold **and** silver are my favorite metals.
Rambo ran up the mountain **and** into the clouds.
The boy standing in the puddle **and** the girl waving a white hanky are Mongo's cousins.
Aphasia went shopping, **but** she couldn't find any frozen oatmeal.

The conjunctions we will be working with most are called **coordinating conjunctions:** *and, but, or, nor, for, yet,* and *so.*

I saw her through the window, **so** I hid under the sofa.
Clean your room, **or** you won't be able to find your bed.
Florene doesn't like aerobics class, **nor** does she enjoy bicycling.
Let's elect Archie, **for** he's a jolly good fellow.
I saw Jason at midnight, **yet** I wasn't afraid.
The ice is melting, **so** skate fast!

Exercise

Please underline the coordinating conjunctions in these sentences:

1. My dog howls at pictures of Lassie and Benji.
2. You went to school, but you forgot your homework.
3. Clorene sprained her ankle, so she can't go parachuting with us.
4. Grandpa Pringle doesn't enjoy movies, nor is he too crazy about television.
5. I fed the goldfish, yet they still raided the refrigerator.
6. Larry, Curly, and Mo joined Mongo and me for cake and squid sherbet.
7. I'd like spaghetti and meatballs or chicken and dumplings for breakfast, please.

SOME WORDS OF CAUTION ABOUT CONJUNCTIONS AND OTHER THINGS

The function of a word in a sentence tells you what part of speech the word belongs to. Most words in isolation can be classified as more than one part of speech; think about the word *rose*, for instance. It can be a noun, as in "The last *rose* of summer is a sad sight." *Rose* can be a verb, too: "We all *rose* to sing the school song." *Rose* can also function as an adjective: "Those *rose* glasses make your eyes look pink." You have to think carefully about what job the word is doing before you can label it.

Look back at page 4, and you'll see *this, that, these,* and *those* in the list of pronouns. They function as pronouns when they appear alone, as in "We bought *this* and *that* at the mall." When *this, that, these,* and *those* point to a noun or pronoun, though, they are doing the work of adjectives: "You take *this* chocolate, and I'll take *that* one."

You'll also notice *his, its* and *their* in the list on page 4, they can also function as adjectives when they are accompanied by a noun: "*His* ragweed is taller than *their* corn."

Conjunctions are especially sneaky in this regard: only when *and, but, or, nor, for, yet,* and *so* are *joiners* can they be called conjunctions. For example, "I love anchovy pizza, so I have it for breakfast" uses *so* as a joiner of two sentences, so it is clearly a conjunction here. Now look at this: "He was *so* handsome that he made me feel dizzy." In this sentence, *so* isn't a joiner; it's an adverb that modifies *handsome.* Here are other examples of words that are sometimes conjunctions, but here are being used for a different job:

She's had nothing **but** trouble since she lost her lucky charm. (**preposition**)
I've got good news **for** you. (**preposition**)
I keep waiting for a miracle; however, nothing's happened **yet.** (**adverb**)

And, or, and *nor* are the only words that are always conjunctions; they are always used as joiners.

EXCLAMATIONS

An **exclamation** simply expresses emotion and has no grammatical relationship with the rest of the sentence. Actually, anything said with enough oomph can function as an exclamation; it's all in how you say it (or write it)!

Rats on a twig! The tractor fell into the well!
Suffering succotash! The canary's attacking the cat!

Words like *yes, no, well,* and *oh* are often used as very mild exclamations; they are followed by a comma. Stronger exclamations, such as the preceding ones, need an exclamation mark (!).

Oh, I don't know whether I want to go skydiving.
Yes, I've packed my parachute.
No, I don't have any other plans.
Well, I just can't decide.

Exercise

Imagine that you are in each of the following situations. Write the exclamation you would use.

1. You have just won the MVP award for your log-rolling team. _____

2. You have just locked yourself out of your apartment for the third time this week. _____

3. You have just discovered that your goldfish can talk. _____

4. You have finally found a parking place, but you don't have any money for the meter. _____

5. You have just been notified that you have won a million golf balls. _____

Parts of Speech Exercise 1

"Yes, I tried to pull the wool over your lovely eyes," Tom said sheepishly, "and I am very, very sorry."

In the sentence above, find as many of the following items as you can. (*Warning!* Perhaps the sentence doesn't contain all of the parts of speech requested; be careful.)

Common Nouns: _____

Proper Nouns: _____

Pronouns: _____

Verbs: _____

Adjectives (including articles): _____

Adverbs: _____

Prepositions: _____

Conjunctions: _____

Exclamations: _____

Parts of Speech Exercise 2

The itsy-bitsy, teeny-weeny, yellow polka-dot linguini upset my poor stomach terribly, so I quickly drank some bright pink Pepto-Bismol under the table.

In the preceding sentence, find as many of the following items as you can:

Common Nouns: _____

Proper Nouns: _____

Pronouns: _____

Verbs: _____

Adjectives (including articles): _____

Adverbs: _____

Prepositions: _____

Conjunctions: _____

Exclamations: _____

Parts of Speech Exercise 3

From your own vocabulary, pick an example, any example, of the following parts of speech:

Common Noun: _____

Proper Noun: _____

Pronoun: _____

Verb: _____

Adjective: _____

Adverb: _____

Preposition: _____

Conjunction: _____

Exclamation: _____

Parts of Speech Exercise 4

Please circle the common nouns in this hauntingly familiar Peony McAllister story:

It was a dark and stormy night, but brave, beautiful Peony McAllister quickly finished her dinner of Swedish meatballs, Russian tea, English muffins, and Norwegian sardines, put on her fuchsia boots, grabbed her frilly umbrella, and made her lonely way through the inky alley. Terrified, she bumped into a huge, water-soaked box, fell over an abandoned skateboard, and leaped over a muddy puddle. Her nervous laughter echoed through the half-empty garage, but her bright brown eyes finally found the object of her frantic search, and, as she kick-started her trusty motorcycle, she gave a loud cheer, glad that she wouldn't be late for her nightly Japanese flower-arranging class.

Parts of Speech Exercise 5

Please circle the adjectives in Peony's continuing saga:

Peony McAllister was so excited about her extremely interesting Japanese flower-arranging class that she completely ignored the bright red stop signs randomly placed here and there on her route to school. Suddenly, her very cold ears picked up the hauntingly familiar sound of a skull-shatteringly loud siren, and she saw dazzling lights in her rearview mirror. Frantically, she began to create convincingly pathetic excuses for going too fast. As she slowly pulled over to the side of the road, she patted her motorcycle tenderly and smiled bravely at the very large person who was slowly approaching.

Test on Parts of Speech

Part I

Identify the part of speech of the *italicized* words in each of the following sentences:

Example: Rambo and *I* walked *our* parakeet.   *pronoun*

1. *Invisible* spiders and *noisy* weevils invaded my garage.   *adj.*
2. *Birds* and *bees* make me sneeze.   *noun*
3. Leroy ran *around* the corner and hid *under* a bush.   *verb*
4. Elroy *ran* around the corner and *hid* under a bush, too.   *verbs*
5. Grandpa Pringle wants *us* to go scuba diving with *him*.   *pronoun*
6. *Golly Ned!* My horse got stung by a bee! *Whoa!*   *exclamation*
7. Ezra *pounded* the steak and then *smothered* it in onions.   *verb*
8. Chively *wearily* placed the buffalo in a *very* large pan.   *adverb*
9. Mongo eats raw garlic *and* onions, *so* he walks alone.   *coord conj*
10. Aphasia barbequed my *shoes* by *mistake*.   *noun*
11. The burglar tiptoed *through* the tulips and ran *into* the raspberry bushes.   *prep.*
12. Mongo *jumped* on the grapes and *ruined* his reputation.   *verb*
13. When Rambo *snarled* at the clock, it *stopped*.   *verb*
14. *Leprechauns* are taller than *elves* but shorter than *gnomes*.   *noun*
15. *Wild* horses couldn't drag me to that *boring* movie.   *adj.*
16. *Magically* and *mysteriously*, the apple pie disappeared *completely*.   *adverb*
17. He washed his red pajamas with his white shirts *and* socks, *so* he's now known as "Pinky."   *coord conj.*
18. *You* and *I* are from New England, but *he* and *she* are from another planet.   *pronouns*
19. The *right* answer will get you a *cheery* smile and a *kind* word.   *adj verb*
20. If you call your *sister* a *dweebazoid* again, I'll be forced to turn you into a *toad*.   *noun*
21. I'm *desperately* seeking Fedonia; have you seen her *lately*?   *adverb*

15

Part II

Please write a sentence that contains a noun, a verb, a conjunction, an adverb, and at least one adjective. Label these parts of speech in your sentence.

_____

_____

SECTION 2 — Sentences and Dependent Clauses

If you can write a good, clear, powerful sentence, you can write anything: term papers, job applications, short stories, novels, plays, movies—whatever you want to write. In this section, you will learn what ingredients make a sentence and how to tell the difference between a sentence and a dependent clause. Exercises will help you sharpen your skills, and a test at the end will tell you how much you have learned. (By the way, the test will also include some items from Section 1, so you can keep using what you have learned so far.)

SENTENCES (OR INDEPENDENT CLAUSES)

Before we launch into clauses, it might be a good idea to learn what a **phrase** is. A phrase is a group of related words that acts as a single part of speech and that lacks a subject (a noun or a pronoun about which something is being said), or a whole verb (one with person, number, and tense), or both. For example, *dancing in the moonlight* is a phrase; there is no subject, nor is there a whole verb—*dancing* is only part of a verb—so it must have help if it's going to do the work of a verb. (If this intrigues you, look at page 101.) If you look back at page 9, you'll notice that the last few words of each of the gorilla examples contained a preposition, an article, and a noun; we referred to these constructions as **prepositional phrases,** which often function as adverbs, telling us when, where, how, and so on. The important thing to remember for now is that a phrase doesn't have both a subject and a whole verb.

A **clause,** however, must have *both* a **subject** and a **whole verb.** An **independent clause** expresses a complete thought. (When it stands alone, an independent clause is usually called a **sentence,** but when it is only part of a sentence it is usually called an independent clause, or, sometimes, a **main clause.**)

Maine has lots of pine trees and potatoes.
(The subject is *Maine,* the verb is *has,* and the group of words expresses a complete thought.)
I like cuddly, fuzzy, affectionate wombats.
(The subject is *I,* the verb is *like,* and the group of words expresses a complete thought.)
Rambo, Rocky, Mongo, Grandma Pringle, and the Houston Astros danced in the street.
(*Rambo, Rocky, Mongo, Grandma Pringle,* and the *Houston Astros* are the subjects, the verb is *danced,* and the group of words expresses a complete thought. By the way, when there is more than one subject, we call it a **compound subject.**)
The bugs in my garden nibbled the nasturtiums, licked the lilies, ate the asters, and spat out the spinach.
(The subject is *bugs,* and the verbs are *nibbled, licked, ate,* and *spat.*
The group of words expresses a complete thought.)
Are the crocodiles and alligators in the bathtub again?
(Questions are sentences. If you juggle the word order around, you'll find that all the requirements are met; the subjects are *crocodiles* and *alligators,* the verb is *are,* and the group of words expresses a complete thought.)

As you can see, a sentence may have several subjects and several verbs. The important thing to remember is that, to qualify as a sentence, a group of words must have at least one subject and at least one verb, and it must express a complete thought.

You might think, then, that a sentence must have at least two words in it, one for the subject and one for the verb. Believe it or not, there are one-word sentences. Smile! When you are issuing commands or making requests, the subject is always understood to be *you,* and it isn't said or written. Therefore, all of the following can be called sentences even though you don't see the subject: Freeze! Please open the window. Go to Helsinki! Jump in the lake! Please jump in the lake. Follow me. Stop that! Go away.

BITS OF FASCINATION ABOUT SUBJECTS AND PREDICATES

You might hear people in the classroom talking about **complete** and **simple subjects,** and, on a clear day, you might hear the word **predicate** being tossed around.

The **simple subject** of a clause is just the stark naked noun or pronoun, with no adjectives or frills, that drives the verb.

The **complete subject** of a clause includes everything that goes along with the noun or the pronoun that drives the verb.

The short, ugly, warty witch turned Lyle into a toad.
(The simple subject is *witch*; the complete subject is *the short, ugly, warty witch*.)
Big, fat, red, juicy apples and golden, slender bananas are my favorite fruits.
(The simple subjects are *apples* and *bananas*. The complete subject is *big, fat, red, juicy apples and golden, slender bananas*.)

The **simple predicate** of a clause is just the stark naked verb.

The **complete predicate** is what is left over when you take away the complete subject.

(In the first example above, the simple predicate is *turned*; the complete predicate is *turned Lyle into a toad*.)
(In the second example, the simple predicate is *are*; the complete predicate is *are my favorite fruits*.)

We won't be doing a lot with predicates, but you'll be glad to know what they are, so you can join the conversation in the classroom.

SOME WORDS OF CAUTION ABOUT SUBJECTS

You have just learned that the subject of a clause must be a noun or a pronoun, but please don't twist that around and think that any old noun or pronoun in the clause is the subject.

The little old lady kicked the football.

You can see that there are two nouns here: *lady* and *football*. They are not both subjects.

Which noun is doing something? The little old *lady* is performing the action, so she is the subject.

Football is the direct object; it is receiving the action.

We'll go more deeply into objects in Section 6, but start being careful now. Figure out the function of the word before you make any hasty decisions about subjects.

DEPENDENT CLAUSES

A **dependent clause** has both a subject and a whole verb, but it *doesn't express a complete thought*; it depends on more information, so it can't stand alone. Dependent clauses are also known as **subordinate clauses** because they are less powerful than independent clauses—they are incomplete. If you said, "While you were napping" to someone, your listener would wait for you to finish; you have said *when* something happened, but not *what* happened. You need to join the dependent clause to an independent clause. "While you were napping, I wrecked your car" does express a complete thought (even though the thought isn't good news to the owner of the car).

There are certain words that *signal* that a **dependent clause** is on the way; here are some of the most common ones:

while	after	although	as if
when	because	as soon as	since
before	though	until	till
where	wherever	if	as
unless	as though	once	rather than

These signal words are technically known as **subordinating conjunctions,** but calling them **signal words** helps us to avoid confusing them with **coordinating conjunctions,** good old *and, but, or, nor, for, yet,* and *so,* which we have already become familiar with. (The coordinating conjunctions join words, phrases, or clauses of equal weight; the subordinating conjunctions join less powerful dependent clauses with independent clauses.)

If a dependent clause comes before the independent clause that completes the thought, use a comma after the dependent clause.

If Mr. Frankenstein marries Miss Dracula, their children will be little monsters.
Because I love you, I will make marshmallow pizza for your dinner.
After he left, we all wept.

No comma is needed if the independent clause comes before the dependent clause.

Their children will be little monsters if Mr. Frankenstein marries Miss Dracula.
I will make marshmallow pizza for your dinner because I love you.
We all wept after he left.

Exercise in Independent and Dependent Clauses

Please write five independent clauses (sentences); underline the simple subject(s) once and the verb(s) twice.

1. _____
2. _____
3. _____
4. _____
5. _____

Write five dependent clauses; circle the signal words, and underline the simple subject(s) once and the verb(s) twice.

1. _____
2. _____
3. _____

4. _____

5. _____

Now add a new independent clause to each of your dependent clauses to make a complete sentence.

1. _____
   _____

2. _____
   _____

3. _____
   _____

4. _____
   _____

5. _____
   _____

Sentence Recognition Exercise 1

Please analyze each of the following groups of words and decide which category it belongs in. Write the letter beside the question number.

A. Incomplete sentence: no subject
B. Incomplete sentence: no verb
C. Incomplete sentence: dependent clause
D. Complete sentence

Examples:

___A___ Broke the washing machine.
(This doesn't tell us who broke the washing machine, so it lacks a subject.)

___B___ Rambo and Mongo
(This doesn't tell us what Rambo and Mongo are doing, so it lacks a verb.)

___C___ Before you wash your hands.
(This has a subject and a whole verb, but the signal word at the beginning keeps it from expressing a complete thought, so it's a dependent clause.)

__D__   You are wonderful.
(This has a subject and a whole verb, and it expresses a complete thought, so it's a complete sentence. Hurrah!)

_____ 1. Students and teachers.

_____ 2. The eight-toed wombat.

_____ 3. Ate all the pizza.

_____ 4. Peony McAllister.

_____ 5. The flower is lovely.

_____ 6. After the snow melted.

_____ 7. Snarled and growled.

_____ 8. When it rains.

_____ 9. Fell up the stairs.

_____ 10. If you go home.

_____ 11. Scared the dog.

_____ 12. This room.

_____ 13. I made some squid sherbet.

_____ 14. Played the kazoo.

_____ 15. Fedonia and I.

MORE ABOUT DEPENDENT CLAUSES

Another kind of word used to introduce dependent clauses is the **relative pronoun:**

who	whose	whom
whoever	whomever	what
whatever	which	that

There's a bit of trickiness here because relative pronouns can also serve as subjects of independent clauses:

Who left the catcher's mitt in the dishwasher?

This is a perfectly fine question; the subject is *who*, the whole verb is *left*, and the group of words expresses a complete thought.
    Look at this, though:

Mom's going to mangle the person **who left the catcher's mitt in the dishwasher.**

Here, the clause describes *person*, and it's functioning as an adjective. It's safe to say that when a relative pronoun isn't starring in a question, it's signaling the beginning of a dependent clause.

OK, hang on to your hat! One last bit of niftiness about dependent clauses is that they can function as adjectives, adverbs, and nouns:

The player **who is on first** swallowed his bubblegum. (**adjective clause**)
He swallowed the bubblegum **when the pitcher beaned him.** (**adverb clause**)
Whoever chews bubblegum during a game is asking for trouble. (**noun clause**)

A FEW WORDS ABOUT KINDS OF SENTENCES

Now that you know about dependent/subordinate and independent/main clauses, you can classify sentences by looking at the clauses they contain.

A **simple sentence** has just *one* independent clause:

I'm weeping.

A **compound sentence** has *at least two* independent clauses:

I'm weeping, and you're laughing.

A **complex sentence** has *at least one independent clause and one dependent clause:*

If you don't stop laughing, you're going to be in big trouble.

A **compound-complex sentence** has *at least two independent clauses and at least one dependent clause:*

I'm weeping because you don't take me seriously, so please stop laughing right now.

Whew! We've been through a lot of information in these few pages. Here's a small exercise just to give you some practice.

Exercise

Write a simple sentence.

Please write a compound sentence. (If you'd like to know how to punctuate it, look at Comma Rule 1 on page 32.)

How about a complex sentence?

_____

Now, for the grand finale, let's have a compound-complex sentence.

_____

Sentence Recognition Exercise 2

For any of the following groups of words that is a complete sentence, write S next to its number; if it is not complete, rewrite it as a complete sentence.

_____ 1. More powerful than a locomotive.

_____ 2. When it's your turn.

_____ 3. Yelled down the well.

_____ 4. That referee.

_____ 5. The patient spider.

_____ 6. If you like blueberry pancakes.

_____ 7. Who is standing on the desk?

_____ 8. Who is standing on the desk.

_____ 9. Over the rainbow.

_____ 10. Motorcycles and lollipops.

_____ 11. The man who came to dinner.

_____ 12. Whispered sweet nothings.

_____ 13. Mother's Day and Halloween.

_____ 14. You are my favorite person.

_____ 15. The smallest planet.

_____ 16. Sweet Georgia Brown.

_____ 17. Tripped over the pot of gold.

_____ 18. Bandits and pirates.

_____ 19. Before you go.

_____ 20. Destroyed the kitchen.

Weird Exercise in Sentence Construction

Select as many words as you like from each category and see how many sentences you can make. Use only the words that appear in the lists, but you may use words more than once. Your sentences may be as wild as you like.

Examples:

1. The very ugly earthworm fell on the purple salad and laughed cheerfully.
2. An empty, wild motorcycle admired the square airplane too often.
3. A thin, happy computer met the sweet elephant, but it went behind the ginger ale and sang shyly.

Articles	Nouns	Pronouns	Adjectives	Verbs	Adverbs	Coordinating Conjunctions
a	elephant	this	short	fell	rather	and
an	motorcycle	that	small	go	very	but
the	salad	who	purple	went	often	or
	flower	whose	wild	is	completely	nor
Prepositions	ginger ale	I	glorious	are	much	for
without	cookie	you	ugly	sang	well	yet
during	chair	he	sweet	felt	too	so
against	robot	she	thin	ate	hastily	
toward	computer	it	happy	drove	shyly	**Signal Words**
at	doctor	we	wide	met	sadly	since
through	airplane	they	square	heard	cheerfully	unless
in	hero	someone	clean	had	silently	because
behind	actress	her	red	found	carefully	when
on	hammer	him	old	sat	lazily	if
to	puppy	us	empty	laughed		while
	earthworm	them	hollow	admired		although

Test on Parts of Speech, Sentences, Clauses, and Subjects

Part I

Please identify the part of speech of the *italicized* word in each of the following sentences:

Example:
I miss my rubber ducky *terribly*.　　　　　*adverb*

1. Superman's mother can see *through* brick walls.　　*prep*
2. Aphasia made a marshmallow meatloaf *for* Mongo.　*c c*
3. Chively Sneed likes candy, *but* he never buys any.　*cc*
4. Haven't you heard about your prize *yet*?　*c c*
5. You have finally gone *too* far, big fella.　*adverb*
6. The balloon *exploded* in the dark.　*verb*
7. You look *rather* weary, dearie.　*adv*
8. The *invisible* spider bit my toe.　*adj.*
9. We buried the treasure, *so* let's make a map.　*cc*
10. *They* are my favorite mechanics.　*pron*
11. Those *tiny* bars of soap keep getting lost.　*adj.*
12. I insulted your canary, so he bit *me*.　*pronoun*
13. The *mouse* ran up the clock and lost all track of time.　*noun*
14. She shrieked when the refrigerator *suddenly* fell over.　*adv.*
15. The angry squirrels *threw* acorns at the doghouse.　*v.*
16. Fedonia's daughter makes music with a frying pan *and* a spoon.　*cc*
17. *An* improbable excuse is better than no excuse at all.　*I.-A.*
18. *Seventy-six* trombones can make a lot of noise.　*Pro.noun*
19. Astronomers *have* stars in their eyes.　*V.*
20. Hockey players have nocturnal *teeth*.　*n.*

Part II

Write a sentence that begins with a dependent clause and contains a noun, a verb, a conjunction, an adverb, and at least three adjectives. Label these parts of speech in your sentence.

_____

_____

Part III

Please analyze each of the following groups of words and decide in which category it belongs. Write the letter beside the question number.

    A. Incomplete sentence: no subject
    B. Incomplete sentence: no verb
    C. Incomplete sentence: dependent clause
    D. Complete sentence

_____ 1. Coughed and sneezed.

_____ 2. Smile!

_____ 3. Rambo and Rambette.

_____ 4. Burning tires smell awful.

_____ 5. Went to sleep.

_____ 6. Unless you help me celebrate.

_____ 7. Fell through the cracks.

_____ 8. Jumped over the fence.

_____ 9. Although you are eccentric.

_____ 10. Silver threads among the gold.

_____ 11. My heart belongs to Grandma.

_____ 12. Duck!

_____ 13. A bicycle built for two.

_____ 14. Aphasia sprinkled tacks on her driveway.

_____ 15. If you get a flat tire.

_____ 16. My foot.

_____ 17. Snakes give me the howling fantods.

_____ 18. Tumbled over the edge.

_____ 19. Is worth its weight in feathers.

_____ 20. When you slice onions.

Part IV

Go back to Part III and make complete sentences out of the items that you put into category A, B, or C.

Part V

In each of the following sentences, write S over the nouns or pronouns that are subjects and V over the verbs.

Example:

    S   V

Rambette took her parakeet for a walk.

1. Invisible spiders and noisy weevils invaded my garage.

2. Leroy and Elroy ran around the corner and hid under a bush.

3. Ezra pounded the steak and then smothered it in onions.

4. Chively wearily placed the buffalo in a very large pan.

5. Mongo eats raw garlic and onions, so he walks alone.

6. Rambo snarled at the clock, so it stopped.

7. Mongo jumped on the grapes and ruined his reputation.

8. You and I are from New England, but he and she are from another planet.

9. Magically and mysteriously, the apple pie disappeared completely.

10. Aphasia barbequed my shoes by mistake.

11. Pinky washed his red pajamas with his white shorts and socks.

12. The burglar tiptoed through the tulips and ran into the raspberry bushes.

13. The right answer will get you a cheery smile and a kind word.

14. Fedonia is lost, but her compass is here.

15. Wild horses dragged the tall leprechauns to the boring movie.

Punctuation

This section will help you learn how to punctuate sentences in order to help your reader understand exactly what you mean. Although you will find twelve comma rules, two semicolon rules, a colon rule, and some advice about quotation marks, hyphens, parentheses, and the dash, we will concentrate in the exercises and test on the three comma rules and the one semicolon rule used most often in writing. You will become so familiar with Comma Rules 1, 2, and 3 and with Semicolon Rule 13 that you won't have to stop and look them up.

By this time, you know in your heart that the test at the end of this section will cover all that you have learned so far.

PUNCTUATION RECOGNITION

Before we get into the uses of specific punctuation marks, let's make sure of their names and forms.

Make the punctuation mark beside its name:

1. Comma
2. Period
3. Apostrophe
4. Colon

31

5. Semicolon   9. Dash
6. Quotation marks   10. Parentheses
7. Question mark   11. Hyphen
8. Exclamation mark

Please name the following marks:

1. ?   _____   7. ( )   _____
2. ,   _____   8. '   _____
3. !   _____   9. —   _____
4. " "   _____   10. -   _____
5. ;   _____   11. .   _____
6. :   _____

COMMA RULE 1

Use a **comma** (,) before *and, but, or, nor, for, yet,* and *so* when the word joins two complete sentences. When these words function as joiners, they are called **coordinating conjunctions.**

①
There were bells on the hill, **but** I never heard them ringing.

Remember that a complete sentence must have a subject and a verb, and it must express a complete thought.
  Do not use a comma before the conjunction if there is not a complete sentence on each side of the conjunction.

Baby gorillas are cuddly **and** adorable.
Victor **and** Virginia found sticks **and** stones in the carburetor.

Exercise

Please circle the conjunctions in the following sentences. If the conjunction joins two complete sentences, insert a Rule 1 comma before the conjunction.

Examples:

①
Peony likes motorcycles, (but) Mongo prefers skateboards.
The casserole contains cabbage (and) cauliflower.

1. Let's clap for the Wolfman for he's going to play our song.

2. Chively built a concrete canoe but it wouldn't float.

3. Rambo and Rambette like to sit around and growl at each other.

4. Mario will win the race or I'll eat my spare tire.

5. My peculiar parakeet doesn't like newspapers nor is he crazy about magazines.

6. You lost the bet so you have to march behind the elephants in the parade.

7. You're trying to gain weight yet you're still eating birdseed salad.

8. George and Martha invited Jim and Dolly over for ice cream and cake but Dolly fell and skinned her knee so they couldn't go.

9. We went camping last week but we forgot the cooler and the tent so we came home early.

10. You did all the digging so the treasure is yours.

HELP WITH RULE 1

If you had trouble with the Rule 1 exercise, try this step-by-step method to determine whether a conjunction is joining complete sentences: put your finger under the conjunction and test each side of it.

Goats love grass and tin cans.

Put your finger under *and*; then look at all of the words on the left side of *and*:

Goats love grass

There is a subject, *goats*; there is a verb, *love*; the group of words expresses a complete thought; therefore, *Goats love grass* is a complete sentence.
   Now look at the right side of *and*:

tin cans.

This doesn't have a verb, nor does it express a complete thought, so *tin cans* isn't a complete sentence.
   Since Rule 1 asks for a comma before a conjunction that joins two complete sentences, you know that you can't use a Rule 1 comma here.
   Just so you can get the hang of this, here's another one:

Zula waltzes beautifully but she tangos terribly.

Put your finger under *but*; then look at all of the words on the left side of *but*:

Zula waltzes beautifully

There is a subject, *Zula*; there is a verb, *waltzes*; the group of words expresses a complete thought; therefore, *Zula waltzes beautifully* is a complete sentence.

Now look at the right side of *but:*

she tangos terribly.

There is a subject, *she;* there is a verb, *tangos;* the group of words expresses a complete thought; therefore, *she tangos terribly* is a complete sentence.

Since Rule 1 asks for a comma before a conjunction that joins two complete sentences, you know that you need a Rule 1 comma here:

          ①
Zula waltzes beautifully, but she tangos terribly.

Use this method until you can instantly see when and where you need a Rule 1 comma.

COMMA RULE 2

Use a comma to separate items (words, phrases, or clauses) in a **series.** A series consists of three or more items.

          ②   ②   ②
Chili contains beans, meat, onions, and peppers.
          ②   ②
Chili gives me hives, heartburn, and hiccups.

Exercise

Please count the items in each of the following sentences. If a sentence contains a series of three or more items, use commas to separate them.

Examples:

              ②   ②
Pauline likes to climb mountains, to explore caves, and to embroider pillowcases.
Pauline enjoys adventure and needlework.

1. Rambo eats nails tacks and staples for lunch.
2. Rambette eats bullets and ball bearings.
3. Mongo crawled through fire and hot oil to be first in line for the movie.
4. Peony's motorcycle coughs sputters and stalls when she tries to start it.
5. Fedonia's pet wombats eat and sleep all day long.
6. Would you like coffee tea or chokecherry juice?
7. Chively's favorite holidays are Halloween Labor Day and Martin Van Buren's Birthday.

8. Snow White made breakfast for Dopey Doc Sneezy and Grumpy.
9. Bashful Sleepy and Happy had already left for the mine.
10. Florene and Clorene collect posters of Larry Curly and Mo instead of Groucho Harpo and Zeppo.

MORE ABOUT RULE 2

Some writers omit the comma before the conjunction that joins the last item in a series, but the comma is never incorrect, and it sometimes prevents confusion.

The elephant landed on the Jackson twins, Terry and Rod.

The reader isn't sure whether there are four or two people under the elephant: are Terry and Rod the Jackson twins, or are Terry and Rod two other people? A Rule 2 comma would clear this up immediately:

②   ②
The elephant landed on the Jackson twins, Terry, and Rod.

The reader can now be certain that there are four people under the elephant.

If you develop the habit of always using a comma before the conjunction in a series, you won't have to worry about puzzling your readers, and they'll be grateful.

You are now familiar with the only situations where a comma appears before a conjunction:

1. When the conjunction joins two complete sentences.
2. When the conjunction joins the last item in a series.

COMMA RULE 3

When a dependent clause begins with a subordinating conjunction (look back at the list of signal words on page 20), use a comma at the end of the dependent clause if it comes before the independent clause.

③
When the cows come home, I'll lock the barn door.
③
While you were out, the phone rang off the hook.

No comma is needed if the dependent clause doesn't come before the independent clause.

I'll lock the barn door when the cows come home.
The phone rang off the hook while you were out.

Exercise

Please examine the following complex sentences very carefully. If the dependent clause comes before the independent clause, put a Rule 3 comma at the end of the dependent clause. Since no comma is needed if the dependent clause doesn't come first, write *OK* beside the sentences that don't need a Rule 3 comma.

Examples:

When I played my electric kazoo in the bathtub,③ I got a shock.

OK I got a shock when I played my electric kazoo in the bathtub.

1. As soon as the bank opens let's apply for a loan together.
2. Let's apply for a loan together as soon as the bank opens.
3. When I found a rattlesnake in the dryer I fainted.
4. I fainted when I found a rattlesnake in the dryer.
5. You'll get a ticket if you park on the sidewalk.
6. If you park on the sidewalk you'll get a ticket.
7. I'll give you some squid sherbet because you're my friend.
8. Because you're my friend I'll give you some squid sherbet.
9. When you go to the store please get some more pickled porcupine.
10. Please get some more pickled porcupine when you go to the store.

Punctuation Exercise

Using Comma Rules 1, 2, and 3, punctuate the following sentences correctly. Put the rule number above each comma that you use. Be careful; some of the sentences might not need commas.

1. Leroy and Elroy are on a new diet.
2. They eat sawdust and drink melted icicles.
3. My boss and her daughter have red hair green eyes and orange noses.
4. I cleaned Mongo's room and then I locked the door so he can't mess it up again.
5. You take the high road and I'll take the bus.
6. Grandma and Grandpa took Aphasia and me to the Cosmic Clashes concert but they said the music was too tame for them.
7. Poor Mongo lost his wallet his car keys and his lucky rabbit's foot.
8. The fish swallowed the hook line and sinker and then started on the lock stock and barrel.
9. Inertia and I won a blue ribbon at the fair but our wombat ate it on the way home.

10. The bus is leaving so run for it!
11. Will you still need me and feed me when I'm sixty-four?
12. When I'm sixty-four will you still need me and feed me?
13. Mrs. Bridges Mr. Udson and Rose live downstairs.
14. If I wear a purple potato sack to the party will you laugh at me?
15. Will you laugh at me if I wear a purple potato sack to the party?
16. Although you are my favorite person I want to be alone.
17. You can catch more flies with honey than with vinegar but what are you going to do with them?
18. Matt is a standup comic so he doesn't own any chairs.
19. There are mice in the walls and termites in the woodwork but it's still my home and I love it.
20. Kate felt guilty when she stayed home from her job with the circus but she was tired of being shot out of a cannon and sawed in half.
21. Peony's favorite colors are puce chartreuse and aubergine but I think they're weird.
22. If you'll put your trombone away I'll tell you a bedtime story.
23. Rambo and Rambette growl and snarl so they don't need large vocabularies.
24. Fedonia's pet lion fell into the paving machine so she calls him Leotarred.
25. Get down jump back and cool out.

COMMA RULE 4

Use a comma to separate adjectives that describe the same noun. (These are called **equal adjectives,** and their positions are interchangeable.)

         ④   ④
The hungry, thirsty termites attacked the flat, wet toothpicks.
(*Hungry* and *thirsty* both describe *termites; flat* and *wet* both describe *toothpicks*.)
         ④   ④
The thirsty, hungry termites attacked the wet, flat toothpicks.
(The position of the adjectives doesn't make any difference here; they are interchangeable.)

     The positions of adjectives involving age, size, color, and number are not always interchangeable; a useful test is to see whether you can insert *and* sensibly between the adjectives. If you can, the adjectives are equal, and you need a Rule 4 comma:

The little old raccoon removed its mask.
(We don't use a Rule 4 comma here because "old little raccoon" sounds weird, and we wouldn't say "little *and* old raccoon.")
The ten big white houses landed in Oz.
(We don't use Rule 4 commas here because "the white big ten houses" sounds weird, and we wouldn't say "the ten *and* big *and* white houses.")

Please be sure to remember that Rule 4 applies *just to adjectives*. Look at this:

④   ④
The fuzzy, ugly, bright green mold in the refrigerator turned out to be a wonder drug. (This is tricky because *bright* here is an adverb describing *green;* if it were an adjective describing *mold,* the mold would then be of above-average intelligence, and that's too terrifying to think about!)

Exercise

Underline the adjectives in the following sentences and use Rule 4 commas to separate adjectives that describe the same noun:

1. The tall awkward stranger stepped on my tired aching foot.
2. The friendly tiger rolled over and revealed his fuzzy fat tummy.
3. The bright purple skateboard took off on its own down the steep winding hill.
4. Stately plump Buck Mulligan made some hot delicious stew.
5. The short chubby porcupine got stuck under the dirty dented truck.
6. The handsome actor swung on the long tangled vines and landed on a crocodile.
7. The hostile sleepy neighbors complained about your wild noisy party.
8. The popular young rock star tripped over his long curly microphone cord.
9. The very sweet little chimpanzee gave me a sticky sour lollipop.
10. The six enormous old pink elephants pranced through my very troubled dreams.

COMMA RULE 5

Use a pair of commas to set off interrupting words or phrases in a sentence.

⑤   ⑤
He will, of course, be late for his dental appointment.
⑤   ⑤
You must, despite the blizzard, go get some vitamins for your giraffe.
⑤   ⑤
Grandma will, as always, tell me to turn my frown upside down.

Exercise

Please insert Rule 5 commas if they are needed in the following sentences:

1. We're running out of ice naturally because of the heat wave.
2. I plan come heck or high water to see that new movie tonight.
3. Aphasia and Inertia however have already seen it twice.
4. They told me despite my protests the whole story.

5. I will therefore hide the last chapter of the suspense novel they're reading.

6. Mongo is according to his mother Mr. Congeniality.

7. He lost his temper though last week.

8. He flew into a ring-tailed snit by golly.

COMMA RULE 6

Use a comma after a participial phrase beginning a sentence. (See page 141 for a complete explanation of participial phrases.)

Embarrassed by the compliment, Peony blushed.

Eating nothing but fish eyelashes, he lost 700 pounds.

Exercise

Look closely at each of the following sentences to see whether it begins with a participial phrase; if so, insert a Rule 6 comma:

1. Stuck in the hula hoop Mr. Jellyby whimpered.

2. Rising to the surface the diver wiped mud from her eyes.

3. Stranded at the mall Clorene and Florene shopped till they dropped.

4. Worried about shortages at the post office Rambo and Rambette started a stampede.

5. Dazzled by my rhinestone earrings the burglar bumped into a chair.

6. We heard a walrus singing in the moonlight.

7. There is a monster lurking in the closet.

8. Her eyes sparkling Lizzo sharpened her wits.

9. Stunned by the thunder the possum played dead.

10. Forgotten by his fans the former football hero wept.

11. Laughing and singing the Bobbsey twins repaired the tricycle.

12. Living in the Midwest I see a lot of spectacular sunsets.

13. Flattened by the boulder the flower wilted and died.

14. Defeated by the Roadrunner the coyote gnashed his teeth.

15. Missing his target the hunter decided to clean his glasses.

COMMA RULE 7 (AND A FEW WORDS ABOUT RESTRICTIVE AND NONRESTRICTIVE ELEMENTS)

Use a pair of commas to set off nonrestrictive elements in a sentence.

In order to make any sense at all of Rule 7, we need to be able to recognize restrictive and nonrestrictive elements, so hang on! **Restrictive elements,** which may be words, phrases, or clauses in a sentence, contain information that is absolutely necessary to the meaning of the sentence. They specify (or restrict) the words they're describing.

The keys to the dungeon were just out of the prisoner's reach.
(The phrase *to the dungeon* tells which keys, so the phrase is restrictive.)
A person who goes to bed early misses a lot.
(The clause *who goes to bed early* specifies the kind of person, so it's restrictive.)

Vagueness would abound if we tried to leave the restrictive elements out of the examples above; we'd have:

The keys were just out of the prisoner's reach.
(Which keys?—car keys? piano keys? answer keys?)
A person misses a lot.
(What kind of person?—a missing person? an important person? any run-of-the-mill person?)

Nonrestrictive elements add interesting detail, but they aren't necessary to the meaning of the sentence, so they *can* be left out.

⑦ ⑦
Mongo's house, which is an oildrum on stilts, needs a new roof.

The clause *which is an oildrum on stilts* isn't absolutely essential; without it, we have:

Mongo's house needs a new roof.

which is OK.

⑦ ⑦
Transylvanian poetry, which some people love, bores me to death.

Without the nonrestrictive clause, we have:

Transylvanian poetry bores me to death.

Do you see how Rule 7 commas are almost like handles you can use to lift the nonrestrictive elements out of the sentence? You have to think very carefully about the elements, especially groups of words starting with *who, whose,* or *which,* before you can decide whether they are restrictive or nonrestrictive.

The lady who is up against the wall is my mother. **(restrictive)**
The lady, who has 108 cats, finally bought a dog. **(nonrestrictive)**

You can make things a bit easier by using *that* to introduce **restrictive elements** and saving *which* for the beginnings of **nonrestrictive elements:**

⑤ⓜ ⓜⓜ

Chocolate pie, which is very fattening, is my favorite breakfast.
Chocolate pie that has been left out in the rain isn't very appetizing.

This is a very useful device, but it can't be used in all situations because using *that* for people is a bit rude:

A man who has been at death's door welcomes each sunrise.
A man, who looked very shiftless, ordered a new transmission from Uncle Lazlo.

It's OK (for reasons of variety or because of writer's cramp) to leave out *who* and *which*, turning a clause into an **appositive,** the technical term for a word or group of words that can take the place of the noun that comes right before it. Appositives can be restrictive or nonrestrictive:

ⓜ ⓜ

Mongo's house, an oildrum on stilts, needs a new roof.
My brother Elmo is studying to be an electrician, but my brother Rambo wants to be a florist.

One more bit of fascination about Rule 7: If the nonrestrictive element comes at the end of the sentence, you need just one Rule 7 comma; the punctuation at the end of the sentence removes the need for the second one.

ⓜ

Go complain to the owner, the lady in the red dress.

ⓜ

Do you live in Illinois, the most beautiful place in the world?

Exercise

Look very carefully at the sentences below. Insert Rule 7 commas around nonrestrictive elements; if a sentence doesn't need Rule 7 commas, write OK beside it.

Examples:

ⓜ ⓜ

That tall man, whose mother is my neighbor, has no left ear.

OK A car that is powered by dust bunnies is my idea of heaven.

1. Mr. Legree the owner of the apartment building loves ferns and petunias.
2. The town philosopher Soda Crates McGurk sits on a cracker barrel.
3. The person who sings before breakfast usually smiles all the time.
4. My grandmother an engineer plays bridge every working day.
5. Monstro Suggins who has 196 pigs collects silk purses.
6. A person who is 105 pounds underweight is usually invisible.
7. This is the house that Jack built.

8. This is my house which needs to be painted.
9. Uncle Elmo the game warden hates poached eggs.
10. The philosopher Plato believed that nothing exceeds like excess.
11. The dog whose mouth is foaming has rabies.
12. I ordered my favorite snack which is albatross-on-a-stick and chokecherry juice at the Miss Tucson diner.
13. The manager of the shoe store said that these are the times that try men's soles.
14. Raquel McClure has a canary that sings four-part harmony.
15. We sent a card to Chively Sneed who's in the hospital because he's allergic to chicken.
16. Jason the leader of the neighborhood kazoo band is tone-deaf.
17. We finally talked to Mr. Ed who was a little hoarse.
18. My mother who was Mrs. America in 1925 still has a radiant smile.
19. Rambette whose sister wears combat boots is my best friend.
20. Please don't eat the daisies that are in the refrigerator.

COMMA RULE 8

Use a comma to set off the names of persons, places, or things being addressed. If the name comes first in a sentence, the comma follows it; if the name comes last, the comma precedes it; if the name appears elsewhere in the sentence, use a comma before and after the name.

Sam, you made the pants too long.

Here I come, California!

Listen here, you rusty bucket of bolts, you'd better not stall.

Exercise

Insert Rule 8 commas wherever they are needed in the following sentences. Be careful!

1. We are here my friends to mourn the passing of my pet python.
2. Please eat your birdseed Tweetie.
3. Mongo I have barricaded your room.
4. Ladies and gentlemen may I have your attention?
5. Today boys and girls we're going to search for elves.
6. Boys and girls searched for elves today.
7. Are you ready for a new star Hollywood?

8. We saw ladies and gentlemen at the kazoo concert.

9. Fedonia Krump come here this instant!

10. My fellow Americans my rubber ducky has sprung a leak.

COMMA RULE 9

Use a comma to set off short words and phrases, such as *yes, no, well, oh, nevertheless, therefore, after all, finally, in conclusion,* etc., when they appear at the beginning of a sentence.

⑨
Yes, we have some bananas.
⑨
Oh, don't you find them appealing?

Exercise

Look very carefully at the following sentences and insert a Rule 9 comma where it is needed:

1. No I'd rather not go to aerobics class in snowshoes.

2. Well let me say this about that.

3. Nevertheless you promised you'd make marshmallow soup today.

4. Finally Rambo and Rambette got their new bazooka.

5. Yes I'll help you housebreak your new wombat.

6. At long last we can go to the flea festival.

7. Therefore we won't be here for your demolition derby.

8. After all there's no place like home.

9. Oh please don't fence me in.

10. In conclusion I'd like to invite you to tour the salt mine.

COMMA RULE 10

Use a comma with *too* when it means *also* wherever it occurs in a sentence. (Look at page 91 if you're wondering what else *too* can mean.)

If *too* comes first, the comma follows it; if *too* comes last, the comma precedes it; if *too* appears elsewhere in the sentence, use a comma before and after it.

⑩
Are you a Taurus, too?
⑩   ⑩
Gerbils, too, can learn to tango.

Exercise

Use Rule 10 commas in the following sentences where *too* means *also*:

1. The cave is dark, and it's smelly too.
2. We too must march with flaming torches to the castle.
3. If Rambette gets a new grenade, I deserve one too.
4. If you get up early, be sure to go to bed early too.
5. You're too wonderful for words.
6. Deacon Porter is too tall to be a jockey.
7. Are your children night owls too?
8. This water balloon is too small, and it's leaky too.
9. If you're too nervous to explore the haunted house, I'll stay home too.
10. Cinderella scrubbed the dungeon and drained the moat too.
11. Are you too turning down the Caesar salad, Brutus?
12. Too we must do our homework before we go to sleep.
13. We too would like some purple cotton candy at the fair.
14. Grandpa loves to waltz, and Grandma does too.
15. Geraniums are pretty, and they smell nice too.

COMMA RULE 11

Use a comma before a conversational question that's added to the end of a statement. (These are questions that are not of life-and-death importance, and the asker usually already knows the answer.)

Peony McAllister is your cousin, isn't she?

They all live in a yellow submarine, don't they?

Exercise

Please insert a Rule 11 comma where it is needed in the following sentences:

1. You're not afraid of the eight-toed wombat are you?
2. Aphasia won the watermelon-juggling contest didn't she?
3. I washed the parakeet last night didn't I?
4. Good fences make good neighbors don't they?
5. The television set overheated and exploded during your favorite program didn't it?
6. Do you know the way to Buzzards Bay?

7. You know the way to Buzzards Bay don't you?

8. Was spring a little late this year?

9. Spring was a little late this year wasn't it?

10. The boss wants us to go home early doesn't she?

COMMA RULE 12

Use a comma to separate words that might be confusing if they were read together. The comma provides a pause for your readers, so they won't have to read the sentence several times to puzzle out what you mean.

    ⑫

After eating, snakes go to sleep.
(Without the comma to stop them, readers might try to cope with *after eating snakes*.)

    ⑫

From you, flowers are always welcome.
(The comma keeps this from saying *from you flowers*.)

Exercise

Please supply a Rule 12 comma wherever it is needed in the following sentences:

1. To begin with diamonds are expensive.

2. To you toads are adorable.

3. To Peggy Sue was very polite.

4. In 1988 999 wombats mysteriously disappeared.

5. In the water lilies are a lovely sight.

6. Whenever possible pit bulls are to be avoided.

7. In this school teachers are often asked for their autographs.

8. As a matter of fact finding Mongo's house is tricky.

9. Walking the dog got as far as the corner.

10. To you perfect people are boring.

A FEW WORDS OF REASSURANCE

Whew! Now that you have lived through twelve comma rules, you may have noticed that some situations give you a choice of comma rules to use.

For instance:

The fearless actress swung on the long, snaky, tangled, unattached vines.
(You have a choice of using either Rule 4 or Rule 2; the adjectives all describe *vines*, so Rule 4 would be appropriate. You have a series of adjectives [three or more], so Rule 2 is appropriate, too.)

The gerbils wanted to go to the concert, too, but the tickets were too expensive for them.
(You have several choices here for the rules governing the commas: Rule 10 because *too*
means *also* here, Rule 5 for the interrupting word *too*, and Rule 1 for the comma before
but.)
Walking on, the hiker paid no attention to the screaming crowd.
(Rule 6 would be correct; *walking on* is an introductory participial phrase. Rule 12 would
be correct, too; the comma keeps readers from being puzzled by *walking on the hiker*.)

It's important to know at least one reason for each comma you use, so you
won't just toss them, like salt and pepper, into your writing. Get into the habit of
asking yourself the reason for each comma you're tempted to use. If you can't think
of a reason, leave the comma out.

SEMICOLON RULE 13

A **semicolon** (;) is stronger than a comma and weaker than a period. Use a semicolon
to join two related, complete sentences when there is no conjunction (*and, but, or,
nor, for, yet, so*) to join them.

It snowed last night⑬ our car is buried today.

The cow is in a bad mood⑬ she's producing sour cream.

Trying to join two industrial-strength sentences with a weak, fragile comma is like
trying to join two steel girders with a piece of wet Scotch tape. A comma must have
a conjunction to help it join sentences; when there is no conjunction, a semicolon
is the punctuation you need. (In case you've heard the terms **comma splice** and
run-on sentence floating around, here's what they mean: a comma splice is the
result of trying to join sentences with a mere comma; a run-on sentence has no
punctuation at all between two or more sentences, which can drive your readers
wild with frustration and confusion. If you replaced the semicolons in the preceding
examples with commas, you'd end up with comma splices. If you removed the semicolons altogether, you'd end up with run-on sentences.)
By the way, the word following a semicolon is not capitalized unless it's a proper
noun, a proper adjective, I, or a pronoun referring to God.

Exercise

Examine each of the following sentences carefully to determine what punctuation
to use. If a conjunction joins two complete sentences, insert a Rule 1 comma before
the conjunction. If there is no conjunction between the two complete sentences, join
them with a Rule 13 semicolon. If there are not two complete sentences, you might
need one of the other comma rules, or perhaps you won't need any punctuation. Be
careful!

Examples:

⑬
The rooster couldn't sleep; he crowed all night long.

①
The rooster couldn't sleep, so he crowed all night long.

1. It rained last night there are puddles everywhere today.
2. It rained last night so there are puddles everywhere today.
3. The teacher was nervous and he dropped the chalk ten times.
4. The teacher was nervous he dropped the chalk ten times.
5. Rambo eats anvils and barbed wire for breakfast.
6. I admire you because you're brave and polite.
7. You're brave and polite I admire you.
8. You're brave and polite so I admire you.
9. Peony and Chively cooked and cleaned Mongo and Fedonia whined and complained.
10. Tuesday is payday so let's celebrate.

A FEW MORE WORDS ABOUT SEMICOLON RULE 13

Some adverbs indicate a very strong relationship between two independent clauses; when they function as joiners, these adverbs are called **conjunctive adverbs;** some of the most-used ones include:

therefore	consequently	besides
moreover	furthermore	in fact
nevertheless	however	indeed
accordingly	likewise	instead
otherwise	thus	still

Because these conjunctive adverbs mark such a strong relationship between independent clauses, a heavy-duty semicolon must appear between the clauses. If the conjunctive adverb comes at the beginning of the second clause, use a comma after the conjunctive adverb (and the semicolon will be before the conjunctive adverb, right between the clauses):

The henhouse roof leaks; however, the hens seem to enjoy showers.

If the conjunctive adverb comes at the end of the second clause, use a comma before it (and the semicolon will remain right between the clauses):

The henhouse roof leaks; the hens seem to enjoy showers, however.

If the conjunctive adverb comes elsewhere in the second clause, use a pair of commas around it (and the semicolon will remain right between the clauses):

The henhouse roof leaks; the hens, however, seem to enjoy showers.

Be careful not to confuse conjunctive adverbs and subordinating conjunctions (the signal words for dependent clauses; you might want to refresh your memory by looking back at page 20). The signal words are *always* first in their clauses and can't skip merrily around the way conjunctive adverbs can.

One more word of caution: don't automatically assume that you're dealing with a conjunctive adverb when you see one of the words on the conjunctive-adverb list; be sure that the adverb is working to join two strongly related independent clauses before you start flinging semicolons around. Look at this:

Despite your many faults, I still love you.
(You don't have two independent clauses here, so *still* is functioning as a plain old adverb.)

Look at this, though:

You have many faults; still, I love you.
(You do have two independent clauses here, and there is a very strong relationship between them, so *still* is functioning as a conjunctive adverb.)

Exercise in Semicolon Rule 13 and Commas with Conjunctive Adverbs

Insert commas and Rule 13 semicolons where they are needed in the following sentences. Be careful; there might be some trickiness.

1. Those fuchsia boots are inexpensive in fact they cost less than a new shirt.
2. Those fuchsia boots are inexpensive they cost less in fact than a new shirt.
3. Those fuchsia boots are inexpensive they cost less than a new shirt in fact.
4. I'm too tired to go skydiving moreover my parachute is torn.
5. I'm too tired to go skydiving my parachute is torn moreover.
6. I'm too tired to go skydiving my parachute moreover is torn.
7. Mongo ordered cottage fries instead of cottage cheese.
8. Are you still waiting for the Great Pumpkin?
9. I am a Taurus therefore you can't change my mind.
10. I am a Taurus you can't therefore change my mind.

SEMICOLON RULE 14

Use a semicolon to separate items in a series when the items already contain commas.

They walked to Hartland, Maine; Charlottesville, Virginia; and Tucson, Arizona.
Dirty Harry had a bath on May 14, 1938; September 30, 1953; and June 6, 1970.

A Rule 14 semicolon isn't restricted to series of dates or addresses. Look at this:

The umpire ejected Spitball Cranston, the pitcher; Paddy Croce, the catcher; and Willie Bob Tantrum, the manager, from the game.

Do you see how the semicolons keep the reader from getting confused? Without the semicolons to separate the people in this series, the reader wouldn't know for sure whether three or six people were tossed out of the game. Because the semicolons separate the people, we know that Spitball Cranston is the pitcher and that the comma is a Rule 7 comma.

Please notice that this is the only situation in which a semicolon appears before a coordinating conjunction.

Exercise

Insert Rule 14 semicolons wherever they are needed in the following sentences. Be careful, though; some sentences might need Rule 2 commas.

1. Fedonia adopted a new wombat in November, 1930 August, 1949 and April, 1973.
2. Rambo and Rambette have destroyed sections of Caribou, Maine Troy, New York and Northampton, Massachusetts.
3. Grandma Pringle has lived at 4092 Silver Street, Carson City, Nevada 681 Dolphin Drive, Miami, Florida 2903 Rook Road, Atlantic City, New Jersey and 666 Beefcake Boulevard, Los Angeles, California.
4. Aphasia wore mittens earmuffs and long underwear to the tiddlywinks tournament.
5. Gloria Muldoon, a radiologist Alvin Krebs, a banker Joan Rio, a juggler and Barbara Doucette, a welder, received awards at the banquet.

COLON RULE 15

The **colon** (:) introduces an explanation or an example.

Use a colon to show that what follows is a fuller explanation of what has been stated.

Julius is tall: he has to bend over to put the basketball through the hoop.

Use a colon before a list of items, especially when the list comes after the words *as follows* or *the following.*

Please pack the following for your camping trip: a tent, a tablecloth, a lawn chair, and a satellite dish.

There's no need to capitalize the word following a colon unless the word is a proper noun, a proper adjective, I, or a pronoun referring to God.

Exercise

Please insert a Rule 15 colon wherever it is needed in these sentences:

1. Please deliver the following at noon tomorrow five tons of gravel, a gallon of insect repellent, an ant farm, and nine caterpillars.
2. Our house has all the modern conveniences electricity, indoor plumbing, screen doors, and a lightning rod.
3. Junior slyly hid the following under his sister's bed snakes, snails, a rat's skeleton, barbed wire, and a live skunk.
4. Our swim team is planning to offer lessons in all the popular strokes the Australian crawl, the backstroke, the breast stroke, and the dog paddle.

QUOTATION MARKS

A. Use **quotation marks** (" ") around the exact words of a speaker (a direct quotation).

Peony said, "I was born to ride my motorcycle."

An indirect quotation doesn't require quotation marks; it uses the word *that*.

Peony said that she was born to ride her motorcycle.

Commas and periods are always inside the end quotation marks.

Peony's mother said, "Please clean your room, dear."
"The road is calling me, so I can't, Mom," Peony replied.

Semicolons and colons are always outside the end quotation marks.

Peony's favorite song is "Engine Ears"; she listens to it every day.

When the quotation is a question or an exclamation, the question mark or exclamation mark is inside the quotation marks.

Peony's mechanic asked, "Do you know the way to Casco Bay?"
Peony yelled, "You bet I do!"

When the quotation is not a question or an exclamation, the question mark or exclamation mark is outside the quotation marks.

Why did Rambette whine, "Snails aren't fast food"?
Hurrah! The boss finally said, "You deserve a raise"!

Notice that a comma comes before the quotation marks in a direct quotation and that the first word in a direct quotation is capitalized.

B. Use quotation marks around the titles of book chapters, magazine articles, poems, episodes of television and radio programs, short stories, and songs.

"The Golden Gate Bridge" is a very suspenseful article.
Our poetry class recited "The Ups and Downs of Elevator Operators."
Did you watch "The Wombat's Winning Ways" on *Nature* last week?
"The Gift of the Magi" is a hair-raising short story.
Grandma Pringle hums "Stardust" when she cleans the telescope.

Underline titles of books, magazines, plays, movies, and newspapers. (This is the equivalent of setting them in italics.)

My very favorite novel is The Broom of the System.
The June issue of Gardener's Eden has a good article about fig leaves.
The Peoria Pork Producers will present their version of Hamlet next month.
Rambette has seen Rambo XXV 137 times.
The Wall Street Journal doesn't have any comic strips.

Use single quotation marks (' ') around a direct quotation within a direct quotation and also around the titles of book chapters, magazine articles, poems, episodes of television and radio programs, short stories, and songs within a direct quotation. (In other words, you can't have double quotation marks within double quotation marks.)

Mrs. McAllister whispered, "When Peony says, 'Suzuki,' I always say, 'Gesundheit.'"
Mongo's mother sighed, "I know that 'Fifty Ways to Love Your Lever' is your favorite article, dear, but you can't paper your room with it."

THE HYPHEN

A. Use a **hyphen** (-) to link words for clarity. Look at this:

Mongo is a new car owner.

Hmmmmmmmm. Does this mean Mongo has a new car or that he's the owner of a car for the very first time? You can use a hyphen to keep your readers from gnashing their teeth in confusion and chaos:

Mongo is a new-car owner.
(It's very clear that Mongo's car is new.)
Mongo is a new car-owner.
(It's very clear that Mongo owns a car for the first time in his life; the car itself might actually be ten years old.)

B. Use a hyphen when you're spelling out a number between twenty and one hundred.

Inertia wants "When I'm Sixty-Four" played at her wedding.

C. Use a hyphen when you run out of room at the end of a line and need to continue a word on the next line.

Chively never knows when to stop when he's spelling "banana."

A dictionary will help you divide words into syllables, so you'll know where to put the hyphen at the end of the line.

PARENTHESES

Use **parentheses ( )** around words or groups of words that give explanatory, by-the-way information that is not absolutely essential to the meaning of the sentence. Parenthetical remarks are closely related to Comma Rule 5 and 7 situations.

Grandma will (as always) tell me to turn my frown upside down.
That tall man (whose mother is my dentist) has no left ear.

When a group of words in parentheses makes a complete sentence, the period comes before the second parenthesis.

The cafeteria will serve Chef's Revenge tomorrow. (Be still, my heart.)

Punctuation marks within the main sentence come after the second parenthesis.

Mongo's house (an oildrum on stilts), Rambo's room (a hole in a hillside), and Aphasia's apartment (a closet on the thirteenth floor) have all been featured in *Better Attics and Cellars.*

Please notice that parentheses always appear in pairs; there's never a situation that calls for one parenthesis.

THE DASH

A **dash (—)** is useful to indicate a sudden break in thought or a summing up.

Friends, Romans, countrymen—is this microphone on?
Faith, hope, and charity—these are virtues that I hope to teach my children.

When an explanation comes first, use a dash, as in the second of the preceding examples; when an explanation doesn't come first, use a colon:

These are virtues that I hope to teach my children: faith, hope, and charity.

A dash is two hyphens long. In handwriting, a dash is a continuous line; on a typewriter, it's two hyphens with no space between and no space separating it from the words before and after it.

FUN AND GAMES WITH PUNCTUATION

Using any appropriate punctuation rule (including what you have learned about quotation marks, hyphens, parentheses, and the dash), punctuate the following paragraph:

When the very large person reached Peony who was pulled over to the side of the road her stomach started to ache and she regretted her speedy dinner of Swedish meatballs Russian tea English muffins and Norwegian sardines. Good evening officer she said cheerfully but she was in fact in turmoil. The very large person slowly removed his sunglasses and Peony started wondering why on such a dark and stormy night sunglasses were needed at all but she decided not to ask. Meanwhile the lights on the vehicle that had parked behind her motorcycle continued to flash and the siren kept screaming too. That's a lovely sequin headband you have there sir Peony said in her very nicest tone. The very large person grunted Yo. Peony admitted that she might have been going just a bit too fast. Yo the very large person grunted again. You see it's almost midnight and the daylilies will expire before I can arrange them artistically for the final exam in my Japanese flower arranging class. Yo the very large person grunted yet again. Wait a minute cried Peony. Didn't I see an article about you in last week's issue of Film Flam the movie magazine? Blushing the very large person looked shyly at the ground. Aw shucks he said. I was just playing with my new flashing lights and skull shatteringly loud siren and I guess I got carried away. You won't tell anybody you saw me will you? Peony of course replied that she would carry his secret to her grave however she did ask for his autograph which he etched with his dagger into the handlebar of her motorcycle. This along with June 6 1960 February 21 1962 and January 20 1964 is one of my favorite days of all time said Peony. The very large person who shall remain nameless but we all know who he is don't we then returned to his flashing screaming vehicle and sped off into the night. Peony gazed lovingly at the autograph that honored her handlebar and then slowly carefully and joyfully continued on her way to the flower arranging final exam where she overwhelmed the teacher by gluing a daylily to her motorcycle and attaching a poem entitled Putting the Petal to the Metal.

Last Exercise in Punctuation Rules 1, 2, 3, and 13 Before the Test

Using Punctuation Rules 1, 2, 3, and 13, punctuate the following sentences correctly. Put the number of the rule above each comma or semicolon that you use. Be careful! Some of the sentences might not need any additional punctuation.

1. Chively hates fried chicken so Fedonia never serves it.
2. Because Chively hates fried chicken Fedonia never serves it.
3. Chively hates fried chicken therefore Fedonia never serves it.
4. Chively hates fried chicken Fedonia never serves it.
5. Fedonia never serves fried chicken because Chively hates it.
6. Peony has studied flower arranging igloo building and fudge making.
7. Peony plans to visit Japan Alaska and Mackinac Island.

8. Peony enjoys studying and traveling.
9. Because Peony enjoys studying and traveling she's very interesting.
10. Peony is very interesting because she enjoys studying and traveling.
11. Peony enjoys studying and traveling so she is very interesting.
12. Peony enjoys studying and traveling she is very interesting.
13. Peony enjoys studying and traveling therefore she is very interesting.
14. Peony enjoys studying and traveling she is therefore very interesting.
15. Peony enjoys studying and traveling she is very interesting therefore.
16. Peony is practically perfect in every way she makes me want to scream.
17. I wish Peony would take a long walk on a short pier I'm not very nice.
18. Inertia Aphasia and Mongo thrive on clutter turmoil and anxiety.
19. Although Inertia Aphasia and Mongo thrive on clutter turmoil and anxiety they manage to get their work done on time.
20. Inertia Aphasia and Mongo thrive on clutter turmoil and anxiety however they manage to get their work done on time.
21. Inertia Aphasia and Mongo thrive on clutter turmoil and anxiety they manage however to get their work done on time.
22. Inertia Aphasia and Mongo thrive on clutter turmoil and anxiety but they manage to get their work done on time.
23. When we have finished this exercise we can take a break.
24. We can take a break when we have finished this exercise.
25. We have finished this exercise so let's take a break.

Test on Punctuation Rules 1, 2, 3, and 13, Sentences, and Parts of Speech

Part I

1. Write a sentence that contains a preposition. Label the preposition.
2. Write a sentence that contains two pronouns. Label the pronouns.
3. Write a sentence that contains three nouns and two verbs. Label them.
4. Write a sentence that contains two adjectives and two adverbs. Label them.
5. Write a sentence that begins with a dependent clause.

Part II

In the sentences you wrote for Part I, circle the subjects and underline the verbs.

Part III

Analyze each of the following groups of words and decide which category it belongs in. Write the letter beside the question number.

A. Incomplete sentence: no subject
B. Incomplete sentence: no verb
C. Incomplete sentence: dependent clause
D. Complete sentence

_____ 1. Smile!

_____ 2. Because you're my friend.

_____ 3. Locked the wombat in the barn.

_____ 4. Peony McAllister.

_____ 5. Grandma Pringle.

_____ 6. Loves to tango.

_____ 7. When elephants fly.

_____ 8. As soon as you can.

_____ 9. The baby is smiling.

_____ 10. My breakfast exploded in the microwave oven.

Part IV

Go back to Part III and make complete sentences out of the items that you put into category A, B, or C.

56 *Punctuation*

Part V

Punctuate the following sentences. If a sentence doesn't need any punctuation, write OK beside the number.

1. Rambo and Rambette have disappeared.
2. Because they have gone it's very quiet around here.
3. It's very quiet around here because they have gone.
4. They have gone so it's very quiet around here.
5. They have gone consequently it's very quiet around here.
6. When they return let's have a party.
7. We'll invite Mongo if he promises to behave himself.
8. If Mongo promises to behave himself we'll invite him.
9. I'll make squid sherbet raspberry pizza and chokecherry juice.
10. If we invite Peony she'll bring her stupid wretched boring handlebar with her.
11. We're all tired of that handlebar so let's hide it.
12. We're all tired of that handlebar therefore let's hide it.
13. We're all tired of that handlebar let's hide it.
14. Peony will rant and rave if we touch her beloved handlebar.
15. If we touch her beloved handlebar Peony will rant and rave.
16. I hate to be yelled at so I guess I won't do anything to Peony's handlebar.
17. I hate to be yelled at I guess I won't do anything to Peony's handlebar.
18. I hate to be yelled at therefore I guess I won't do anything to Peony's handlebar.
19. I guess I won't do anything to Peony's handlebar because I hate to be yelled at.
20. Because I hate to be yelled at I guess I won't do anything to Peony's handlebar.

4 Sentence Variety, Sentence-Combining, and Sentence-Writing

This section includes some advice about adding variety to your sentences and about combining short, choppy sentences to make longer, more interesting ones. You will also write some sentences about specific topics in order to make use of all you have learned so far about sentence construction and punctuation.

SENTENCE VARIETY AND SENTENCE-COMBINING

Beware of using the basic sentence pattern (subject–verb–object) all the time. Your readers will quickly become bored, and the point you are trying to make will escape them. Variety in your sentences keeps the attention of your readers. There are several ways to combine short, choppy sentences into longer, more interesting ones. Here are three ways:

Use a comma and a conjunction (*and, but, or, nor, for, yet, so*).

Use a dependent clause.

Use a semicolon.

Look at this:

You are a terrific person. I like you a lot.

Here are some ways to combine these sentences.

You are a terrific person, and I like you a lot.
You are a terrific person, so I like you a lot.
Because you are a terrific person, I like you a lot.
I like you a lot because you are a terrific person.
You are a terrific person; I like you a lot.
I like you a lot; you are a terrific person.

Exercise

Please combine the following short sentences into one sentence:

1. Our dog howls all night. Our cat snarls all day. Our neighbors are moving.
2. The car was speeding. The car got a flat tire. The car went off the road.
3. I went to the fair yesterday. I ate cotton candy. I ate soft pretzels. I ate candied apples. I drank four cups of lemonade. I went on the Ferris wheel. I got sick.
4. My boss had a meeting last week. It lasted all morning. Nobody got any work done.
5. The wombat got caught in the drainpipe. The wombat got caught in the drainpipe again. The wombat belongs to Elmo. Elmo removed the drainpipe.
6. The goldfish eats only dandelion seeds. It is winter. Dandelion seeds are scarce. The goldfish is very thin.
7. I plan to make squid stew for dinner. There is no squid in the house. I'll have to go to the store to get some.
8. The canary is big. The canary is fat. The canary is mean. The canary lives next door. The canary bent the bars on its cage. This happened this morning. The canary flew into my kitchen. I was making toast. The canary tore my apron to shreds.

Now that you've had some practice in sentence-combining, you can apply the same principles to the sentences you create. You might jot down several short sentences about a topic and then combine the most promising ones for an effective sentence. See how this works for you in the following exercises.

Sentence-Writing Exercise 1

Using well-chosen words in well-chosen order, create one sentence about each of these topics:

1. Why a college education is necessary for a happy life.
2. Why a college education is not necessary for a happy life.

Take as much time as you need to refine and polish your sentences. Write as many rough drafts as you wish; then write the sentences that you're most pleased with.

Sentence-Writing Exercise 2

Using well-chosen words in well-chosen order, create one sentence about each of these topics:

1. An advantage of living in an apartment.
2. A disadvantage of living in an apartment.

Take as much time as you need to refine and polish your sentences. Write as many rough drafts as you wish; then write the sentences that you're most pleased with.

Sentence-Writing Exercise 3

Using well-chosen words in well-chosen order, create one sentence about each of these topics:

1. A good aspect of television programming.
2. A bad aspect of television programming.

Take as much time as you need to refine and polish your sentences. Write as many rough drafts as you wish; then write the sentences that you're most pleased with.

Sentence-Writing Exercise 4

Using well-chosen words in well-chosen order, create one sentence about each of these topics:

1. The most difficult aspect of being a child in today's world.
2. The most joyous aspect of being a child in today's world.

As always, think about each of these topics carefully and take as much time as you need to refine and polish each of your sentences. Your sentences should interest your readers and make them wish that they could discuss the topics with you. When you're pleased with what you've written, copy each sentence carefully.

Please save your best sentences and look at them again when you're in Section 9.

5 *Singulars, Plurals, Possessives, and Contractions*

In the sentence "Cinderella scrubbed the dungeons' walls," how many dungeons are involved? One dungeon? More than one dungeon? This section will help you straighten out difficult questions like this, and it will also clear up uncertainties about sheep, salaries, deer, and witches.

As always, there is a fascinating test at the end of this section to show you how much you have learned and what (if anything) you'll need to review.

SINGULARS AND PLURALS

A noun or pronoun is **singular** when it refers to one person or item.

boy	girl	captain
teacher	elephant	I
egg	class	giraffe
it	rainbow	apple
soldier	book	dog

61

A noun or pronoun is **plural** when it refers to more than one person or item.

boys	girls	captains
teachers	elephants	we
eggs	classes	giraffes
they	rainbows	apples
soldiers	books	dogs

Most nouns in English form their plurals by simply adding s to the singular.

boy + **s** = **boys** (more than one boy)
tree + **s** = **trees** (more than one tree)
rainbow + **s** = **rainbows** (more than one rainbow)

Nouns (both common and proper) that end in *s, sh, ch, x*, and *z* need an *e* before the plural *s* in order to make the plural form of the word possible to pronounce; the *es* provides another syllable.

one witch	ten witches
one dress	ten dresses
one bush	ten bushes
one box	ten boxes
one buzz	ten buzzes
one Jones	ten Joneses

MORE ABOUT SINGULARS AND PLURALS

The plural of common nouns ending in *y* following a consonant is formed by changing the *y* to *i* and adding the ending *es*. (Consonants are all the letters of the alphabet except *a, e, i, o*, and *u*, which are vowels.)

Suppose you want to form the plural of *salary*. When you look carefully at the end of the word, you will notice that the *y* follows *r* (a consonant), so you change the *y* to *i* and add *es* to get *salaries*.

If the final *y* follows a vowel, you do not change the *y*; to form the plural, simply add *s* to the word: *toy* + *s* = *toys*.

This doesn't apply to proper nouns:

There are 15 Sammys in our family.
The Flannerys are our enemies.

The plural of most nouns ending in *f* is formed by changing the *f* to *v* and adding *es*.

one knife	nine knives
one wife	eight wives
one loaf	seven loaves
one scarf	six scarves
one leaf	five leaves

For some strange reason, *roof, proof, belief, safe*, and *chief* don't follow this rule, so you have *roofs, proofs, beliefs, safes*, and *chiefs*; if you have any theories about why this is so, please let me know, so I can get a good night's sleep.

Some nouns have the same form for both singular and plural:

one deer	nine deer
one trout	eight trout
one sheep	seven sheep
one moose	six moose
one fish	five fish

Here's more trickiness: *each, either, neither, somebody, someone, nobody, no one, anybody, anyone, everybody*, and *everyone* are singular words in precise written and spoken English.

Each of the cowboys **is** going to get **his** own cow.
Either of the mink coats **looks** fine to me.
Everyone is going to the ceremony.
Is anybody home?

Words ending in *ics* might look plural, but they are usually singular:

Physics is fun; mathematics is marvelous; electronics is exciting; politics makes strange bedfellows.

TRICKY PLURALS

Some nouns (usually those derived from Greek and Latin) have irregular plurals that do not follow the usual pattern for plural formation.

Singular	Plural
crisis	crises
thesis	theses
analysis	analyses
appendix (of a book)	appendices
index	indices
phenomenon	phenomena
alumnus (male)	alumni
alumna (female)	alumnae
hypothesis	hypotheses
datum	data
bacterium	bacteria
medium	media
criterion	criteria
stimulus	stimuli
stratum	strata

Here are a few more common nouns with irregular plurals:

Singular	Plural
ox	oxen
child	children
goose	geese
mouse	mice
man	men
woman	women
tooth	teeth
foot	feet
louse	lice

Exercise in Singulars and Plurals

Please examine each of the following nouns carefully to determine whether it is singular or plural. Write *S* or *P* beside the number. If the word is singular, write its plural beside it; if the word is plural, write its singular form beside it.

Examples:

mouse P   mice
flies S   fly

_____ 1. ladies

_____ 2. rainbows

_____ 3. man

_____ 4. birds

_____ 5. loaves

_____ 6. brush

_____ 7. child

_____ 8. women

_____ 9. losses

_____ 10. woman

_____ 11. oxen

_____ 12. glasses

_____ 13. lady

_____ 14. toys

_____ 15. waitresses

_____ 16. moose

_____ 17. children

_____ 18. emergencies

_____ 19. buzzes

_____ 20. churches

_____ 21. witches

_____ 22. sheep

_____ 23. medium

_____ 24. teeth

_____ 25. crises

_____ 26. baboons

_____ 27. monkeys

_____ 28. turkeys

_____ 29. goose

_____ 30. phenomenon

SINGULAR POSSESSIVES

To form the **possessive** of a singular noun, simply add an apostrophe (') and *s*.

the girl's balloon = the balloon belonging to the girl
the monkey's paw = the paw belonging to the monkey
the man's pajamas = the pajamas belonging to the man

Don't worry if the singular form of the noun already ends in *s*; to make the noun possessive, add '*s*.

the waitress's smile = the smile belonging to the waitress
the fortress's walls = the walls belonging to the fortress
Mr. Jones's pet alligator = the pet alligator belonging to Mr. Jones

Exercise

Please form the possessive of each of the following singular nouns:

1. woman _____   6. child _____

2. ox _____   7. goose _____

3. desk _____   8. country _____

4. boss _____   9. pen _____

5. mirror _____   10. glass _____

Now use the *singular possessive form* of each of the preceding nouns in a sentence.

_____

_____

_____

_____

_____

_____

_____

_____

_____

_____

PLURAL POSSESSIVES

To form the plural possessive of a noun, first form the plural; if the plural ends in s, merely add an apostrophe after the s.

singular	plural	ending	add	plural possessive form
boy	boys	s	'	boys'
boss	bosses	s	'	bosses'
country	countries	s	'	countries'
church	churches	s	'	churches'

If the plural does NOT end in s, add an 's to form the plural possessive.

singular	plural	ending	add	plural possessive form
goose	geese	not s	's	geese's
ox	oxen	not s	's	oxen's
child	children	not s	's	children's
woman	women	not s	's	women's

Exercise

Following the pattern just discussed, complete the following:

	singular	plural	ending	add	plural possessive form
1.	analysis				
2.	woman				
3.	child				
4.	mother				
5.	box				
6.	dress				
7.	monkey				
8.	salary				
9.	foot				
10.	sheep				
11.	mouse				
12.	house				
13.	pencil				
14.	book				
15.	cry				

Now use the *plural possessive form* of each of the preceding nouns in a sentence.

_____

_____

_____

_____

_____

_____

_____

_____

_____

_____

_____

_____

_____

_____

CONTRACTIONS

A **contraction** is a short way of saying or writing something. In written contractions, an apostrophe shows that some letters and/or spaces have been omitted.

They're going to be late = They are going to be late.
She's the best boss I've ever had = She is the best boss I have ever had.

SOME WORDS OF CAUTION ABOUT CONTRACTIONS

Please be sure to put the apostrophe in the exact place occupied by the letters in the full form of the word; if you contract *were not*, for example, the apostrophe takes the place of the *o* in *not*, so you end up with *weren't*.

For some reason, the contraction *willn't* doesn't exist; the contraction for *will not* is *won't*, which seems weird, but we have to live with it. (Maybe, though, if you start saying *willn't* and can persuade your family and friends to say it, too, it will catch on—that's actually how the language works!)

Some contractions can be short for different forms; *it's* is the contraction for *it is* or *it has*; *who's* is the contraction for *who is* or *who has*. Once you have become familiar with verbs in Section 7, you won't even think of becoming confused by a contraction ending in *'s*; for now, just remember that you might have the contraction for *is* or *has*.

Exercise

Please form contractions of the following:

1. do not _____
2. I am _____
3. you have _____
4. he is _____
5. we are _____
6. they are _____
7. does not _____
8. they could have danced _____
9. she might have seen _____
10. I should have gone _____
11. it will _____
12. who is _____

13. who has _____
14. it is _____
15. it has _____
16. he cannot _____
17. the taxi is _____
18. she will not _____
19. she would not _____
20. Fedonia is _____
21. it did not _____
22. I should not _____
23. they could not _____
24. he has not _____

Exercise

Please write out the full form of the words contracted below:

1. can't _____
2. haven't _____
3. you're _____
4. he's _____
5. we're _____
6. we'll _____
7. they've _____
8. they're _____
9. don't _____
10. it's _____
11. you've been _____
12. it'll _____

13. weren't _____
14. doesn't _____
15. who's _____
16. didn't _____
17. that's _____
18. Rambo's _____
19. the teacher's _____
20. he'd _____
21. they could've gone _____
22. I might've died _____
23. she should've seen _____
24. who's been sleeping _____

HOW TO TELL THE DIFFERENCE BETWEEN POSSESSIVES AND CONTRACTIONS

Once you get the hang of it, it's easy to tell the difference between a possessive and a contraction; don't let the apostrophe bewilder you.

If the noun or pronoun with the apostrophe in it serves as the simple subject of the sentence, it's part of a contraction. In fact, the contraction frequently gives you both the simple subject and the verb (or at least part of the verb).

Peony's polished her motorcycle five times this morning.
(*Peony* is the subject of the sentence, so you know that you have a contraction for *Peony has.*)
Peony's motorcycle twinkles in the sunshine.
(The subject of this sentence is *motorcycle*, so *Peony's* is possessive: the motorcycle belongs to her.)

Exercise

Look carefully at the *italicized* words in the following sentences. If the word is possessive, write *P* beside the number; if the word is part of a contraction, write *C* beside the number. Please identify the simple subject of each sentence, too.

1. *Cinderella's* been scrubbing the dungeon all morning. Simple subject: _____

2. *Cinderella's* knees are sore. Simple subject: _____

3. The *boy's* lonely. Simple subject: _____

4. The *boy's* loneliness makes him shy. Simple subject: _____

5. The *queen's* crown is missing. Simple subject: _____

6. The *queen's* upset. Simple subject: _____

7. The *wombat's* fur is wet. Simple subject: _____

8. The *wombat's* feet are dirty. Simple subject: _____

9. The *wombat's* not very nice to be near. Simple subject: _____

10. *Mongo's* going home next week. Simple subject: _____

11. *Mongo's* suitcase is covered with dust and cobwebs. Simple subject: _____

12. *Mongo's* been visiting us for two years. Simple subject: _____

13. *Mongo's* definitely worn out his welcome. Simple subject: _____

14. That *play's* very strange. Simple subject: _____

15. That *play's* author writes upside down. Simple subject: _____

THE THIRD USE OF THE APOSTROPHE

You have seen that:

1. the apostrophe indicates the possessive form of nouns:

the bee's knees = the knees belonging to the bee
the kazoo players' club = the club belonging to the kazoo players

2. the apostrophe appears in contractions:

We're all eager to take the exam. = *We are* all eager to take the exam.
Rambo *doesn't* smile very often. = Rambo *does not* smile very often.

The apostrophe and *s* are also used to form the plural of letters of the alphabet, numbers, symbols, and words referred to as words.

There are four **i's,** four **s's,** and two **p's** in Mississippi.
Chively got three **64's** and two **59's** when he bowled last week.
I think **+'s** are prettier than **−'s.**
There are too many **really's** in your sentence.

Exercise

Form the plural of the following weird things:

1. 4 _____   7. s _____

2. 73 _____   8. q _____

3. = _____   9. fantastic _____

4. * _____   10. % _____

5. # _____

6. antidisestablishmentarianism _____

A FEW WORDS ABOUT LITTLE THINGS THAT MEAN A LOT

Use *who* instead of *that* or *which* to refer to people.

slightly rude: Students **that** sit in the back row usually know all the answers.
polite: Students **who** sit in the back row usually know all the answers.

Don't begin a brand-new sentence with a conjunction. A conjunction, after all, is a joiner within a sentence, so it isn't quite logical to use a joiner to start a new sentence. If this is one of your favorite habits, try hitching the sentence you have begun with a conjunction to the sentence immediately before it (using a Rule 1 comma, of course).

blah: Fedonia wants to go to Death Valley for vacation. But I want to go to Dollywood.

better: Fedonia wants to go to Death Valley for vacation, but I want to go to Dollywood.

Please don't abbreviate little words like *and* (&), *through* (thru), *minutes* (mins), *hours* (hrs), and *seconds* (sec). This hurts your readers' feelings by implying that you can't be bothered to take the time to spell the word out for them.

Some abbreviations are clear to everyone: U.S.A., U.S.S.R., Y.M.C.A., m.p.h., etc. In doubtful cases, though, don't abbreviate before you have written out the full name of something; this gives your readers a clue about what the abbreviation means.

If the National Collegiate Athletic Association replaces football with frisbee, angry football fans will march with flaming torches to NCAA headquarters.

The American Automobile Association helps people plan car trips, but there are no roads in the Allagash region of Maine, so the AAA can't give me a road map.

Always spell out numbers one through ten:

I have two canoes, four rowboats, and three catamarans.

Don't mix figures and spelled-out numbers in the same sentence; follow the rule for the larger number:

Peony visited 25 cities in 6 days.
Inertia visited two cities in nine days.

Don't start a sentence with a figure (it's impossible to capitalize figures); if a number begins a sentence, spell it out:

Fifty-three soggy wombats marched through my kitchen last night.

If a number appears in a title, spell it out:

Grandma Pringle's favorite song is "When I'm Sixty-Four."

SOME HANDY SPELLING HINTS

Words spelled with *ie* and *ei* trouble many writers. If you've always had a hard time with words like *niece* (or is it *neice*?) and *receive* (*recieve*?) and *neighbor* (*nieghbor*?), the following rules and their exceptions may help you.

Use *i* before *e* to form the sound of long *e* (the *e* in *me* has the sound of long *e*), except after *c*.

Niece has a long *e* sound, so it is spelled with *ie. Receive* also has a long *e* sound, but it comes after *c*, so it's spelled with *ei.* Here are some more examples:

relieve	ceiling
grief	deceit
believe	conceive

There are also some notable exceptions to this rule:

seize
inveigle (an interesting word meaning to lure or coax)
either
weird
leisure
neither
caffeine
protein
sheik (properly pronounced *shake*, so it's not really an exception to the *ie* rule, but many people mispronounce it)

Use *e* before *i* after *c* and when the sound is *not* long *e*:

neighbor

weigh

seismograph

height

sovereign

Exceptions to this rule are *financier, fiery, mischief, friend, sieve, view,* and *kerchief.*

I hate to tell you this, but proper nouns don't always follow these *ie/ei* rules, so you can't rely on them for help with names like Neil and Sheila, for example.

Here's another fascinating spelling fact that might come to your rescue. Although *argue, nine, true, judge,* and *acknowledge* end in *e*, the *e* is dropped in the following:

argument
ninth
truly
judgment
acknowledgment

(*Judgement* is primarily British, and the dictionary offers it as a second spelling. You now know a handy way to remember the preferred spelling.)

Test on Parts of Speech, Sentences, Punctuation Rules 1, 2, 3, and 13, and Singulars, Plurals, Possessives, and Contractions

Part I

Big, fat, ugly, invisible spiders live in a corner of the garage; they are impatiently waiting for Halloween, so they can dance the eight-leg polka.

In the preceding sentence, find as many of the following items as you can:

Common nouns: _____

Proper nouns: _____

Pronouns: _____

Verbs: _____

Adjectives: _____

Definite articles: _____

Indefinite articles: _____

Adverbs: _____

Prepositions: _____

Conjunctions: _____

Exclamations: _____

Part II

1. Write and punctuate a sentence that uses a Rule 1 comma.

_____

_____

_____

2. Write and punctuate a sentence that uses a Rule 13 semicolon.

_____

_____

_____

3. Write and punctuate a sentence that begins with a dependent clause.

_____

_____

_____

4. Write and punctuate a sentence that uses a series.

_____

_____

_____

5. Write and punctuate a sentence that ends with a dependent clause.

_____

_____

_____

Part III

Please label the simple subject(s) and the verbs in each of the sentences you created for Part II.

Part IV

Please examine each of the following nouns carefully to determine whether it is singular or plural. Write *S* or *P* beside the number. Then, if the word is singular, form its plural; if the word is plural, write its singular form in the blank beside it.

1. child _____   6. scarf _____

2. church _____   7. fox _____

3. monkey _____   8. ox _____

4. toys _____   9. mice _____

5. salary _____   10. women _____

Part V

Please form the possessive of each of the following singular nouns; then use the singular possessive form in a sentence:

1. Europe   _____

2. horse   _____

3. box   _____

4. glass   _____

5. man   _____

Part VI

Please form the possessive of each of the following plural nouns; then use the plural possessive form in a sentence:

1. turkeys   _____

2. ladies   _____

3. men   _____

4. cars   _____

5. children   _____

Part VII

Please form the contraction for each of the following items; then use the contraction in a sentence:

1. who is   _____

2. did not   _____

3. it is   _____

4. they are   _____

5. who has seen   _____

6. it has been   _____

7. Arizona is   _____

8. the snake is   _____

9. they have seen   _____

10. was not   _____

Part VIII

Look carefully at the *italicized* words in the following sentences. If the word is possessive, write *P* beside the number; if the word is a contraction, write *C* beside the number.

1. *Fedonia's* wombat ran away.

2. *Fedonia's* been looking for it in all the wrong places.

3. *Fedonia's* terribly worried.

4. *Peony's* offered to help Fedonia look for her wombat.

5. *Peony's* motorcycle can climb mountains and swim rivers.

6. *Rambo's* going to help Fedonia look, too.

7. If they find the wombat, they'll put it in *Rambette's* helmet.

8. *Rambette's* not too thrilled about having a wombat in her helmet.

9. *Rambette's* got a bee in her bonnet, so a wombat in her helmet shouldn't bother her too much.

10. *Fedonia's* wombat finally turned up at the Last Chance Diner.

Pronouns, Tricky Words That Sound Alike, Double Negatives, and Needless Repetition

When you were young, you might have whizzed into your kitchen with a friend one day and smelled the mouthwatering aroma of freshly baked cookies. Perhaps you tugged on your mother's apron and said, "Me and Kenny would like a cookie, please." Your mother leaned over until her eyes were level with yours, and she replied, "Kenny and *I* would like a cookie, please." Thus, you learned that you get cookies when you say *I* instead of *me*. Your mother was right, of course. *I* is certainly the correct form of the pronoun to use in this situation. You'll be surprised to learn that *me* is correct in the majority of other pronoun situations, though. This section will help you learn when to use *I* and when to use *me*, and it will also help you tell the difference between words like *it's* and *its*. You will find out how to avoid double negatives and needless repetition, too. Read on!

SUBJECT PRONOUNS

Only these forms of personal pronouns may be used as **subjects:**

I   (the person who is speaking or writing)
you   (the person or persons being spoken to)

he	(one male person or animal)
she	(one female person or animal)
it	(one thing or animal of unspecified sex)
we	(more than one person speaking or writing)
they	(more than one person, animal, or thing)

All of these sentences have pronouns as subjects:

I like squid sherbet.
You are my favorite person.
He collects ginger-ale bottles.
She plans to walk to Missouri.
It eats butterfly wings and bee eyelashes.
We bought some seashells at the seashore.
They want to tour New England on unicycles.

Exercise

Replace the *italicized* words in these sentences with the appropriate subject personal pronoun:

1. Georgia Brown offered to keep the kids for a week; *Georgia Brown* is sweet.
2. Florene, Clorene, and Aphasia wrote to me last week; *Florene, Clorene, and Aphasia* are my former neighbors.
3. The peach pie is fresh; *the peach pie* was baked ten minutes ago.
4. Chively Sneed is allergic to chicken, so *Chively Sneed* eats a lot of fish.
5. Rambo and Rambette like picnics because *Rambo and Rambette* can throw grenades at the ants.

OBJECT PRONOUNS

Only these forms of personal pronouns may be used as **objects:**

me	it
you	us
him	them
her	

Please notice that the subject and object forms of *you* and *it* are the same.
    The pronouns in the following sentences are objects:

The Cosmic Clashes played a song for **me.**
Just between **you** and **me,** this party is a real snore.
Do invisible spiders still give **you** the howling fantods?
The class elected **him** Chairperson of the Parade Cleanup Committee.

Grandma Pringle's pet crow sings **her** a lullaby every night.
Peony McAllister rode **it** into the sunset.
Please leave the worrying to **us.**
The sheriff warned **them** for the last time.

The object personal pronoun is needed when the pronoun is the **direct object** of the verb. The direct object receives the action of the verb.

The skunk sprayed **me.**
(The word that receives the action of *sprayed* is *me*, so *me* is the direct object.)

The object personal pronoun is also needed when the pronoun is the **indirect object.** The indirect object shows *to whom* or *for whom* the action of the verb is done. (The prepositions *to* and *for* are often understood before indirect-object pronouns, so you don't always see them.)

The singer gave **her** a come-hither look.
(The word that shows to whom the come-hither look was given is *her*, so *her* is the indirect object here.)

Finally, the object personal pronoun is needed when the pronoun follows (is the **object of**) a preposition.

Fedonia refuses to have anything to do with **them.**
(*Them* is the object of the preposition *with.*)

Perhaps you have heard people say "between you and I"; you now know why that isn't terrific: *between* is a preposition, so you have to use the object form of the pronoun—*me, him, her, us,* or *them*—after it.

Exercise

Please replace the *italicized* words in the sentences below with the appropriate object personal pronouns.

1. Florene is in a snit because the trophy didn't go to *Florene.*
2. Mongo is a skilled firefighter, so let's elect *Mongo* to the Hall of Flame.
3. Aphasia and Inertia played the spoons very well, so give *Aphasia and Inertia* a round of applause.

Exercise in Subject and Object Personal Pronouns

Look carefully at the pronouns in the sentences below. If the pronoun is a subject, write *S* beside the number; if the pronoun is an object, write *O* beside the number.

_____ 1. Please give me a break.
_____ 2. You are the sunshine of my life.

———— 3. Peanut butter makes him itch.

———— 4. Fedonia threw it away.

———— 5. It was my favorite thing.

———— 6. Fedonia didn't consult me.

———— 7. She is no longer my friend.

———— 8. Please don't smile at her.

———— 9. I can't chew this steak.

———— 10. It is tougher than a boiled owl.

———— 11. The judge will always remember them.

———— 12. They shouldn't have laughed in traffic court.

———— 13. Chively won't go to the movies with us.

———— 14. The dark makes him nervous.

———— 15. He doesn't like popcorn.

———— 16. You look confused.

———— 17. Please direct all questions to me.

———— 18. I work for a terrific company.

———— 19. It manufactures kazoo silencers.

———— 20. Please buy one for him.

———— 21. We have never been to Aruba.

———— 22. It looks harmless.

———— 23. The wombat followed her to the store.

———— 24. The teacher expects you to work hard.

———— 25. You have finished for today.

ANOTHER PLACE FOR THE SUBJECT PRONOUN

You have probably heard someone say, "I am younger than her" or "Grandpa is smarter than me." Think about this for a minute; is the object pronoun correct in these circumstances?

Actually, what's going on in these sentences is a form of shorthand: the second verb is understood to be a repetition of the first verb, so it isn't written out or spoken. What the sentences are really saying is:

I am younger than she (is).
Grandpa is smarter than I (am).

Once you are aware of this, it's easy to see that you usually need the subject pronoun after *than.*

Here is an exercise for practice, so you'll be comfortable with this.

Exercise

Choose the correct pronoun for these sentences:

1. He has more freckles than (her   she).
2. You got here faster than (he   him).
3. Wayne and Gordie can play hockey better than (we   us).
4. Mac has more tennis shorts than (me   I).
5. E.T. has better telephone manners than (them   they).

PRONOUNS IN MOB SCENES

Sometimes people get confused about whether to use the subject or the object pronoun when there are a lot of people in a sentence.

Should you say

Captain Kangaroo, Little Lulu, the Queen Mother, the Denver Nuggets, and **me** went to the concert

or

Captain Kangaroo, Little Lulu, the Queen Mother, the Denver Nuggets, and **I** went to the concert?

If a mob scene like this makes you unsure of which form of the pronoun to use, just ignore the rest of the crowd and concentrate upon the pronoun. You certainly wouldn't say

Me went to the concert. (Only Tarzan could get away with that.)

You certainly would say

I went to the concert.

Now that you are sure that you want the subject pronoun, add the rest of the original crowd:

Captain Kangaroo, Little Lulu, the Queen Mother, the Denver Nuggets, and **I** went to the concert.

Should you say

We skydivers have nerves of steel

or

Us skydivers have nerves of steel?

You wouldn't say "Us have nerves of steel." Therefore, you should say, with the utmost confidence,

We skydivers have nerves of steel.

Whenever extra words make you uncertain about which form of the pronoun to use, toss the extra words aside until you have the pronoun straight; then, when you are sure, toss the extra words back in.

MORE MOB SCENES

Would you say

Uncle Ivan gave a present to Peony and **I**

or

Uncle Ivan gave a present to Peony and **me?**

Don't let Peony throw you off; kick her out until you are sure that you want the object pronoun—*me*—and then let Peony back into the sentence:

Uncle Ivan gave a present to Peony and **me.**

Would you say

The astronaut gave **we** fans her autograph

or

The astronaut gave **us** fans her autograph?

When in doubt, toss the extra words out; you would say

The astronaut gave **us** her autograph.

OK, now that you're sure that you need the object pronoun, toss *fans* back in:

The astronaut gave **us** fans her autograph.

Pronoun Exercise

From the choice of pronouns in parentheses, circle the one(s) whose use is correct for the sentence.

1. (Us   We) little old ladies wear parachutes.
2. You're supposed to ride in the van with Jim, Dolly, George, Martha, and (she   her).
3. He's a much more patient Trivial Pursuit player than (me   I).
4. Please come to the State Fair with (he and I   him and me).
5. The boss gave Chively and (I   me) the day off.
6. (He and she   Him and her) are next-door neighbors.
7. Just between you and (I   me), Rambo is a lousy cook.
8. (Us   We) members of the Squid Squad are fearless and brave.
9. There was a shark swimming between (him and me   he and I).
10. (He and I   Him and me) will never go to that beach again.
11. You are much more conscientious than (her   she).
12. Mama writes to Mongo and (I   me) every week.
13. Mongo and (I   me) wish she would telephone instead.
14. (We   Us) nice guys are too polite to suggest it.
15. Papa and (she   her) might move in with (we   us) homeowners because they're tired of their apartment.
16. (We   Us) homeowners might move without telling anyone.
17. You and (she   her) are my best friends.
18. I'd be lost without you and (she   her).
19. There is a strong resemblance between (him and her   he and she).
20. (He, she, we, and they   Him, her, us, and them) work very hard; will there be a bonus for (he, she, we, and they   him, her, us, and them)?

THEM

As you now know, *them* is an object pronoun referring to more than one person, animal, or thing.

The tennis champ collects trophies, and her father dusts **them. (direct object)**
Give **them** the benefit of the doubt. **(indirect object)**
Leave the driving to **them. (object of a preposition)**

Them is obviously never an adjective and can't be substituted for *the, these,* or *those.* Therefore, you would never say or write:

Them blue suede shoes are collectors' items.

You would say:

Those blue suede shoes are collectors' items.

or

These blue suede shoes are collectors' items.

or

The blue suede shoes are collectors' items.

POSSESSIVE PERSONAL PRONOUNS

No apostrophes appear in the possessive form of personal pronouns.

You will recall that the possessive forms of nouns involve strategically placed apostrophes. Apostrophes appear in personal pronouns only when the personal pronouns are parts of contractions:

It's a beautiful day in the neighborhood. = It is a beautiful day in the neighborhood.
It's been raining for weeks and weeks. = It has been raining for weeks and weeks.
You're quite a piece of work. = You are quite a piece of work.

Look carefully at these possessive forms:

my, mine	My giraffe is tame; the tame giraffe is mine.
your, yours	Your canary is fierce; the fierce canary is yours.
his	His house is purple; the purple house is his.
her, hers	Her ranch is huge; the huge ranch is hers.
its	The steer blew its horns.
our, ours	Our neighbors are weird; the weird neighbors are ours.
their, theirs	Their house is on stilts; the house on stilts is theirs.

Notice that *its', your's, her's, our's,* and *their's* don't exist; since apostrophes appear in personal pronouns only when the personal pronouns are parts of contractions, there is nothing on this planet that these forms could possibly mean.

Exercise

From the choice in parentheses, circle the form of the pronoun that is correct for its use in the sentence.

1. Don't hold (you're   your) breath.
2. (They're   Their) silver Mercedes is tarnished.
3. Are those fuzzy dice (your's   yours)?
4. Mighty Mouse crashed into (their   they're) swimming pool.

5. The stuffed moose is (hers   her's).
6. (Their   They're) peacock is prouder than (your's   yours).
7. The nicest house on the street is (their's   theirs).
8. The oldest house on the street is (ours   our's).
9. (It's   Its') been a long time since I had a strawberry frappe.
10. The capon fluffed (it's   its) feathers before the axe fell.

ANOTHER TRICKY PRONOUN

Have you ever been confused about *who* and *whom?*

For some strange reason, *whom* seems to scare the socks off everybody except butlers in old British movies.

Who is the subject form:

Who is knocking at my door?

Whom is the object form:

For **whom** is the bell tolling today?

All the useful things that you have just learned about subject and object personal pronouns apply to *who* and *whom.*

The possessive form of *who* is *whose:*

Whose hubcaps are in the bathtub?

Who's is a contraction that means either *who is* or *who has:*

Who's still knocking at my door? = Who is still knocking at my door?
Who's been using the microwave? = Who has been using the microwave?

Exercise

From the choice in parentheses, circle the form of the pronoun that is correct for its use in the sentence.

1. To (who   whom) did you send your letter of complaint?
2. (Who   Whom) wrote back to you?
3. (Whose   Who's) sorry now?
4. (Whose   Who's) handkerchief is full of sad, salty tears?
5. (Whoever   Whomever) drives to the party will need a map.
6. With (who   whom) do you plan to go?
7. For (whom   who) did you buy the potato chips?
8. (Who's   Whose) going to explain the fire in the bathroom?

9.   (Who   Whom) wants to go to the library with me?
10. (Who's   Whose) the clown (who   whom) filled my car with balloons?

ANTECEDENTS

Antecedent is a handy word to use when you're talking about pronouns: a pronoun's **antecedent** is the word or group of words that the pronoun is replacing. This is known as **pronoun reference.**

Mongo didn't clean his room; he is in a lot of trouble.
(*He* is replacing *Mongo*, so *Mongo* is the antecedent of the pronoun *he*.)
Florene and her sister made their car out of soup cans.
(*Florene and her sister* is the group of words that *their* is replacing, so *Florene and her sister* is the antecedent of *their*.)

If a pronoun's antecedent is singular, the pronoun must be singular; if a pronoun's antecedent is plural, the pronoun must be plural. This is known as **pronoun agreement.** Improper pronoun agreement can drive a reader straight up the wall with confusion:

Grandma Pringle enjoys knitting and embroidering, but it bores me.
(Whoops! *knitting and embroidering* = plural, but *it* = singular; the pronoun has to be fixed before this sentence can mean anything.)
Grandma Pringle enjoys knitting and embroidering, but **they** bore me.
The semicolon is a useful piece of punctuation, but they make me nervous.
(Whoops again! *the semicolon* = singular, but *they* = plural.)

We have a choice of ways to fix this:

The semicolon is a useful piece of punctuation, but **it** makes me nervous.

or

Semicolons are useful pieces of punctuation, but **they** make me nervous.

Pronouns can serve as antecedents for other pronouns, and here's where some trickiness comes in:

Everybody should make up his own mind.
Everybody should make up her own mind.
Everybody should make up his or her own mind.
Everybody should make up his/her own mind.
Everybody should make up her/his own mind.

As you'll recall from page 63, *each, either, neither, somebody, someone, nobody, no one, anybody, anyone, everybody,* and *everyone* are singular words in precise English. This means that when they serve as antecedents for other pronouns, those pronouns should be singular, too.

Look at the choices we have in the preceding examples. If we choose "Everybody should make up his own mind," our pronoun is singular to match the singular antecedent, but we're suggesting that everybody is male; if we choose "Everybody should make up her own mind," we're suggesting that everybody is female. We can avoid this awkwardness and discomfort by choosing "Everybody should make up his or her own mind," "Everybody should make up his/her own mind," or "Everybody should make up her/his own mind." These very clearly include both males and females in "everybody." In your writing, these forms are useful to avoid offending anyone. If they seem long and bulky to you, you might consider changing the antecedent from singular to plural: "All of the *voters* should make up *their* own minds," "All of the *students* should make up *their* own minds," or "All of *us* should make up *our* own minds." We have time when we're writing to think things through and to select the precise words to say what we mean; when we're speaking, however, we often don't have the time to weigh each word, and it would be bulky and bumpy to say "his or her," "his slash her" (that's how we'd have to say "/"), or "her slash his." Therefore, in the interests of smooth, flowing, conversational English, you'll hear people say, "Everyone should make up their own mind," and that has become acceptable in spoken English in all but the most formal situations, so don't leap for the speaker's jugular and scream, "wrong, wrong, wrong!" It does save time, and it avoids offense. Try not to use a plural pronoun with a singular antecedent when you're writing, though.

If the antecedent is unmistakably male or female, always use the pronoun of the appropriate gender, of course:

Each cow has **her** favorite part of the pasture.
Each bull has **his** favorite shade of red.

SOME WORDS OF CAUTION ABOUT PRONOUNS

Unless you're very careful, your readers might get confused about who's who in your writing:

Amylizzo told her mother that she was mistaken.
David can ride with Jimbo, but he'd better get here on time.

Don't these make your hair hurt? Who was mistaken?—Amylizzo or Amylizzo's mother? Who had better get here on time?—David or Jimbo?

You owe your readers a clear sentence, so you will have to do some tinkering. In situations where someone is saying something, you can use a direct quotation:

Amylizzo told her mother, "I was mistaken."
Amylizzo told her mother, "You were mistaken."

In some circumstances, you may choose to repeat the noun instead of replacing it with a pronoun:

David can ride with Jimbo, but David had better get here on time.
David can ride with Jimbo, but Jimbo had better get here on time.

One more handy hint: try not to shift pronouns just for the fun of it in the middle of a sentence; your readers might get confused and lose interest in what you're saying to them:

In the olden days, **we** children had to walk to school through six-foot snowdrifts, and when **we** got there, **you** had to thaw **your** feet beside the pot-bellied stove.

Since the first subject pronoun is *we*, let's stick with *we* throughout the sentence; there isn't any reason to change to *you*:

In the olden days, we children had to walk to school through six-foot snowdrifts, and when we got there, **we** had to thaw **our** feet beside the pot-bellied stove.

Exercise in Pronoun Agreement

Please circle the correct pronoun from the words in parentheses and circle the pronoun's antecedent, too.

1. Each king has always had (his   their) own crown.
2. Although you enjoy blackened cottage cheese for dinner, (it makes   they make) me queasy.
3. Neither Matthew nor Mark brought (his   their) backpack.
4. Each actress has (their   her) own dressing room.
5. Dick and Jane lost (his   her   their) little sister at the mall.

MYSELF

If you have been on an airplane lately, you have probably heard a flight attendant say something like "Captain Ahab and myself have been overjoyed to have you with us aboard Ferguson Airlines." The flight attendant wasn't sure whether to say "Captain Ahab and *I*" or "Captain Ahab and *me*" and hoped to avoid the entire problem by saying "Captain Ahab and *myself*." Nice try, flight attendant, but no jelly doughnut! The flight attendant should have taken a deep breath, tossed Captain Ahab out of the sentence temporarily, realized that the subject pronoun would be correct, yanked Captain Ahab back into the sentence, and said, with the utmost confidence, "Captain Ahab and *I* have been overjoyed to have you with us aboard Ferguson Airlines."

Myself, yourself, himself, herself, itself, ourselves, yourselves, and *themselves* are **reflexive pronouns** that indicate that the subject and object are the same. Reflexive pronouns are never used as subjects, but they are very useful for emphasis:

The mayor **herself** thinks City Hall is dreary.
The show's director **himself** thought the script was wretched.
I want to do it **myself,** Mother!

Reflexive pronouns are also absolutely precise when you want to show clearly that the subject and object in a sentence are the same.

Mongo ran through the screen door and strained **himself.**
I looked in the mirror at dawn and almost scared **myself** to death.
(The subject and direct object are the same person.)
She's going to sit right down and write **herself** a letter.
(The subject and the indirect object are the same person.)
On slow days, **my answering machine** talks to **itself.**
(The subject and the object of the preposition are the same entity.)

Please don't even think of using *hisself, theirselves,* or *ourself*—they aren't considered acceptable.

Exercise in Reflexive Pronouns

From the choice in parentheses, please circle the correct form of the pronoun.

1. Please fly with Captain Ahab and (me   myself) again soon.
2. Norman and (myself   I) plan to open the Bates Motel next week.
3. The neighbors seem very nervous around Norman and (myself   me.)
4. I'm very proud of (me   myself); I haven't had any bubblegum for two weeks, five days, nine hours, and eight minutes.
5. You should be ashamed of (yourself   you); you fell in the well again.
6. Rambette bought (her   herself) a new bowie knife.
7. Chuckles climbed into the clown costume and made a fool of (hisself   himself).
8. The Three Stooges (theirselves   themselves) will march in our parade.
9. Dad bought new bikes for Muffy and (myself   me).
10. Mildew McSwine shot (hisself   himself) in the foot again.

TRICKY WORDS THAT SOUND ALIKE (HOMOPHONES)

Now that you're familiar with contractions and with the possessive forms of personal pronouns, the following tricky words should cease to be tricky. These are words that confuse many people; they sound exactly alike, but you can see that they are very different when they are written (and now you know why).

it's = it is or *it has*

The apostrophe in *it's* shows that some letters have been left out to make one short word.

It's too late to watch the news.
It's taken me five weeks to get here by skateboard.

its = belonging to it

Its is the possessive form of the pronoun *it*.

The machine went berserk and ate its tape, its cord, and its volume switch.

you're = you are

The apostrophe in *you're* shows that some letters have been left out to make one short word.

You're too nifty to be forgotten.

your = belonging to you

Your is the possessive form of the pronoun *you*.

Your vicious canary will end up in jail.

they're = they are

The apostrophe in *they're* shows that some letters have been left out to make one short word.

They're the noisiest people in the neighborhood.

their = belonging to them

Their is the possessive form of the pronoun *they*.

They want their own way.

there = in that place

Please sit there until the interviewer is ready for you.

(*There* is also handy at the beginnings of sentences: *There* is a fly in my soup, but I'm a vegetarian.)

MORE TRICKY WORDS

who's = who is or who has

The apostrophe in *who's* shows that some letters have been left out to make one short word.

Who's the boss?
Who's been driving my Roadmaster?

whose = belonging to whom

Whose is the possessive form of *who.*

Whose turn is it to hose down the kitchen?

to = toward

To is a preposition.

Go to Helsinki!

(*To* is also the first half of the **infinitive form** of a verb: "I like *to surf.*" Stay tuned for Section 7!)

too = also

I'm a hockey fan, too.

too = excessively

Wilt the Stilt is too tall to be a jockey.
He moves too fast for the naked eye to see.

(Handy hint: when *too* means *excessively,* it always appears right before an adjective or an adverb.)

Tricky Words Exercise

From the choice in parentheses, circle the word that is correct for the meaning of the sentence. Take your time, and think carefully about what each word means before you circle your choice.

1. (Your You're) my best friend, so may I borrow (your you're) car?
2. The house was robbed of (its it's) stereo, (its it's) video player, and (its it's) burglar alarm.
3. (You're Your) entitled to (you're your) opinion, but I live here, (to too).
4. (Who's Whose) brave enough to bathe the pythons when (they're there their) hungry?
5. (There Their They're) is (to too) much sin in Cincinnati.
6. (Its It's) after midnight, so I guess (they're there their) not coming.
7. (Whose Who's) house is being used for the party, and (whose who's) going to be there?

8. (Its It's) (to too) bad that (your you're) canary chased (they're there their) cat up a tree.

9. (They're There Their) landlord lowered (they're there their) rent, so (they're there their) very happy; they've lived (they're there their) for eight years.

10. (Its It's) snowing (to too) hard for (you're your) wombat to find (its it's) way home.

11. I'd like (to too) go (to too) Graceland, (to too), but (its it's) (to too) far (to too) ask (your you're) mother (to too) drive us.

12. (Who's Whose) Winnebago is blocking the driveway, and (who's whose) going to volunteer to move it?

13. (It's its) not (to too) great an idea to let Mongo eat (to too) much cotton candy before he rides the Frightmobile.

14. (It's its) been (to too) tempting (to too) look at the last page of the detective story, but I won't ruin (your you're) fun by telling you (whose who's) body was found in the chandelier.

15. The wombats wanted (to too) learn (to too) dance, (to too), but the samba was (to too) fast for (there their they're) stubby little legs.

DOUBLE NEGATIVES

Double negatives actually do the opposite of what the writer intends:

$$\overset{-}{\text{Nobody}} \; \text{did} \; \overset{-}{\text{nothing.}}$$

Nobody did nothing.

This can turn your mind into a pretzel because it really means that somebody did something. The two negatives mingle mysteriously to make a positive. If you've ever read a sugarless gum package carefully, you've noticed that the gum is "not non-caloric." This is a sly way of letting you know that there are calories in the gum even though there is no sugar. To avoid accidental positives, remember that only *one* component of a clause may be negative:

$$\overset{-}{\text{Nobody}} \; \text{did} \; \overset{+}{\text{anything.}}$$

Nobody did anything.

$$\overset{-}{\text{He}} \; \text{didn't do} \; \overset{+}{\text{anything.}}$$

He didn't do anything.

$$\overset{+}{\text{Everybody}} \; \text{did} \; \overset{-}{\text{nothing.}}$$

Everybody did nothing.

A construction like this would be perfectly fine:

$$\overset{-}{\text{We're not}} \; \text{going to the movies because the babysitter} \; \overset{-}{\text{didn't}} \; \text{arrive.}$$

We're not going to the movies because the babysitter didn't arrive.

As you can see, there are two clauses here:

‒

We're not going to the movies

and

‒

because the babysitter didn't arrive.

We're allowed one negative per clause, so we're OK.

MORE ABOUT DOUBLE NEGATIVES

Most negative words begin with *n*: *nothing, never, no, not* (and its contraction, *n't*), *none, nobody, no one,* and *nowhere.* However, there are a few negative words that look innocently positive:

hardly
scarcely
barely

Beware of constructions like this:

I can't hardly hear you.
(This means that I can hear you just fine.)

To get the degree of difficulty or impossibility you want, you can choose

+   ‒
I can hardly hear you.
(This suggests that the voice is faint, and there's difficulty.)

or

‒

I can't hear you.
(This means that the voice is not coming through at all—hearing is impossible.)

You always have the choice of making everything else in the clause positive or of omitting the *hardly, scarcely,* or *barely* altogether, depending on what you really want to say. *Hardly, scarcely,* and *barely* all add an impression of difficulty to your meaning, and they should be used with caution.

STILL MORE ABOUT DOUBLE NEGATIVES

Have you ever heard or read something like this?

‒   ‒

The rock star can't help but attract crowds.
(You guessed it! There's a double negative here!)

The easiest way to fix a *can't help but* double negative (which television newscasters seem particularly fond of) is to toss out the *but* entirely and to follow the *help* with the *ing* form of the verb (technically, the present participle—stay tuned for Section 7 again):

The rock star can't help attracting crowds.

Exercise in Double Negatives

Look closely at the following sentences; if you find a double negative, fix it:

Example:

Mongo didn't do nothing.

Corrected versions:

Mongo didn't do anything.
Mongo did nothing.

1. I haven't never seen a purple cow.
2. There isn't no cranberry juice in the refrigerator.
3. She didn't say anything.
4. I didn't see him across the crowded room, and he didn't see me.
5. Grandpa Pringle can scarcely skydive these days.
6. Grandma Pringle can't hardly twirl her baton.
7. My mother hasn't never been to Australia.
8. I can't help but love my dog.
9. He is nothing but a hound dog, and he cries all the time.
10. I can barely get dressed by myself.
11. My birthday isn't nothing special, so don't go to no trouble.
12. I couldn't help but weep when there wasn't no surprise party.
13. They dug up the beach, but they didn't find no treasure.
14. There has never been such a glorious sunset.
15. Mongo's not going nowhere.
16. I can't hardly look at another garbanzo bean.
17. Senator Mudhen can't help but get into trouble.
18. I looked for some gold under the rainbow, but I could find none.
19. Lizzo isn't scarcely old enough to drive, but she owns a bulldozer.
20. You aren't going nowhere with that flat tire.

Another Exercise in Double Negatives

Please create your own sentences for each of these negative words:

1. no _____

2. can't help _____

3. never _____

4. nowhere _____

5. hardly _____

6. scarcely _____

7. nothing _____

8. no one _____

9. barely _____

10. none _____

REDUNDANCY (NEEDLESS REPETITION) AND WORDINESS

Unless you pay attention to the meaning of each word that you write, it's sometimes easy to use words that say exactly the same thing, which wastes your readers' time and, sometimes, even insults them:

Tinkerbelle's plane leaves at 7 A.M. in the morning.

This is really saying that Tinkerbelle's plane leaves at 7 in the morning in the morning—*A.M* is the abbreviation for *ante meridiem*, which is Latin for "before the midpoint of the day," which is noon. (*Post meridiem*, which means "after the midpoint of the day," is abbreviated *P.M.*) Therefore, if you say "*A.M. in the morning*," you're repeating yourself for no reason, or, worse, you're suggesting that your readers don't know what *A.M.* means, which insults their intelligence. We have a choice of ways to fix the Tinkerbelle sentence:

Tinkerbelle's plane leaves at seven o'clock in the morning.

or

Tinkerbelle's plane leaves at 7 A.M.

Here's another one:

Sergeant Thursday asked for the true facts.

When you think about this carefully, you'll realize that there is no such thing as a false fact. A fact is a statement of truth, so *true facts* will either waste your readers' time or insult them by suggesting they don't know the meaning of *fact*. We can fix this in either of two ways:

Sergeant Thursday asked for the facts.

or

Sergeant Thursday asked for the truth.

Try to avoid wordiness by using the fewest, clearest words possible for what you want to say. The popular phrase "at this point in time" means, when you come right down to it, "now." By saying "now," you could save four words, and your readers would grasp your meaning immediately. "In that time frame" means "then." How about "in a very real sense," which refuses to die? It's hard to think of something in a very *un*real sense. "In a very real sense, I like your purple wombat" means "I really like your purple wombat." Just for fun, suppose you got this note from your child's teacher:

During our recreational time frame, Mongo relates to his peers in a zealously pugnacious manner; their encounters with him frequently result in contusions.

You might be very pleased until you figure out that the teacher is saying that Mongo is beating up his classmates at recess.

Exercise

Look at the following sentences, think carefully about what each word means, and mercilessly chop out unnecessary words.

1. The snake's hissing was barely audible to the ear.
2. The mustard stain on my shirt is scarcely visible to the eye.
3. The glass bowl magnifies the fish and makes them look bigger.
4. At that point in time, I was in seventh grade.
5. In a very real sense, you're making terrific progress.
6. When you open an account at Ferguson Federal, you'll get a free gift.
7. Leave out and omit any unnecessary marshmallows you don't need.
8. Combine anchovies and peanut butter together for an unusual salad.
9. This is the last and final announcement of our sale on wombat houses.
10. Please repeat the address again.
11. Mongo reports for duty at 8 P.M. at night.
12. Please meet me under the clock at McDonald's at 12 noon.
13. Fedonia's stuffed animals dance and sing at 12 midnight.
14. In my opinion, I think leather earrings are nifty.
15. *The Broom of the System* is a popular bestseller.

Test on Just About Everything So Far

Part I

Please identify the part of speech of each of the italicized words in this paragraph:

It was a dark *and* stormy night, but brave, beautiful *Peony McAllister* quickly finished her dinner of Swedish meatballs, Russian tea, English muffins, and *Norwegian* sardines, put on her fuchsia boots, *grabbed* her frilly umbrella, and made her lonely way *through* the inky alley. Terrified, *she* bumped into a huge, water-soaked box, fell over an abandoned skateboard, and leaped over a *muddy* puddle. Her nervous laughter echoed through the half-empty garage, but her bright brown eyes *finally* found the object of her frantic search, and, as she kick-started her trusty motorcycle, she *gave* a loud *cheer*, glad that she wouldn't be late for her nightly Japanese flower-arranging class.

Part II

Using Punctuation Rules 1, 2, 3, and 13, combine the following short sentences into one longer, more interesting sentence. Write the Rule Number above each comma and semicolon you use.

1. Jason bought a mask. Jason bought the mask at the mall. The mask is very scary. The mask makes Jason look like a crazed hockey player. Jason wore the mask yesterday. All the dogs in the neighborhood howled. All the dogs in the neighborhood hid under beds. The owners of the dogs also owned the beds.

_____

_____

_____

2. Raspberry jam is sweet. Raspberry jam is sticky. I dropped some raspberry jam in my typewriter. This happened last week. This was an accident. Everything I type now has marks on it. The marks are red. Everything I type is covered with ants.

_____

_____

_____

3. Mongo is an instructor. Mongo teaches aerobics. Mongo works on Mondays. Mongo works on Wednesdays. Mongo works on Fridays. Mongo works from sunrise till noon. Mongo is in excellent physical condition.

_____

_____

_____

Part III

Please use each of the following constructions in a separate sentence.

Examples:

> *Him and her:* Please give him and her some birthday cake.
> The plural of *sheep:* Ten sheep jumped over the fence and disappeared.

1. The plural possessive of *woman* _____
2. The contraction for *the lady is* _____
3. The plural of *salary* _____
4. The singular possessive of *man* _____
5. *He and I* _____
6. The singular of *media* _____
7. The plural of *child* _____
8. *themselves* _____
9. *whose* _____
10. *its* _____
11. *it's* _____
12. *who's* _____
13. *their* _____
14. *hardly* _____
15. *nothing* _____
16. The plural possessive of *monkey* _____
17. *you and them* _____
18. *too* _____
19. The plural of *box* _____
20. The plural possessive of *box* _____
21. The plural of *leaf* _____
22. The plural possessive of *leaf* _____
23. The contraction for *the flower is* _____
24. The singular possessive of *waitress* _____
25. The plural possessive of *waitress* _____

Part IV

In each of the following sentences, please circle the correct word(s) from the choice in parentheses:

1. Grandma Pringle is more experienced than (me   I).
2. (Whose   Who's) been jumping on (their   they're   there) car?
3. The Great Pumpkin will visit (we   us) true believers.
4. (Who   Whom) did the butler murder on page 492?
5. (Who   Whom) murdered the butler on page 493?
6. Just between you and (I   me), taxes will go down next year.
7. I (can   can't) hardly wait to see (you're   your) new video.
8. Please let (Begonia and I   Begonia and me   me and Begonia) ride with you to Tucson.
9. The sun will rise at (5:45   5:45 A.M.) tomorrow morning, but my son (will   won't) scarcely have gotten to bed by (then   that point in time).
10. (They're   Their   There) upset because the bank promised them a (gift   free gift) for opening an account, but the bank didn't keep (it's   its) word.
11. With (whom   who) will you fly to Washington, Senator?
12. The Cosmic Clashes (have   haven't) never given a concert in (you're   your) hometown, have they?
13. My favorite rock group is the Howling Skitters; they always perform at (midnight   twelve midnight).
14. Have you heard the (untruth   false untruth) about Tarzan and Jane?
15. Grandma Pringle is (to   too) patient with Mongo; she hugs him a lot, (to   too).
16. (It's   Its) been a long time since the car had (it's   its) engine tuned.
17. Don't tell (Peony and I   Peony and me) anything in confidence; (us   we) finkazoids (can   can't) never keep a secret.
18. (She and I   Her and me   Me and her) don't have (any   no) friends.
19. (You're   Your) (to   too) nice to be forgotten; (they're   there   their) (to   too) mean to be remembered.
20. Lizzo likes living in the (city   urban city), but Lulu prefers the (country   rural country.)

Verbs

This section will concentrate on many and various verbs. There are regular verbs and irregular verbs, active and passive verbs, transitive and intransitive verbs. There are moods of verbs. There are action verbs and linking verbs; there are infinitives and auxiliaries. You will learn how to *conjugate* verbs; *conjugation* merely means taking a verb through all the forms it can have in a certain tense.

Suppose a mischievous child announced, "Daddy, I bringed a frog home from the pond and throwed him in the washing machine." If you were Daddy, you'd probably mention the irregular behavior *and* the irregular verbs. Read on!

SUBJECT-VERB AGREEMENT

A verb must match its subject; a plural subject requires a verb in the plural form, and a singular subject requires a verb in the singular form. We say that a verb must agree in *person* and *number* with its subject.

A verb in the **first person** indicates that the subject is either *I* or *we*; the **second person** means that the subject is *you*; the **third person** means that the subject is someone or something other than *I*, *we*, or *you*. For example, *Bob, Ted, Caroline, Alicia, rainbows, marshmallows, he, she, it,* or *they* would all require the third person form of the verb.

The *number* of a verb means simply singular or plural. **First person singular** is the form of the verb that matches the subject *I*; **first person plural** is the form of the verb that matches *we*. **Second person singular** refers to the form of the verb when the subject is *you* (meaning an individual person); **second person plural** is the form of the verb when the subject is *you* (meaning several people). **Third person singular** is the form of the verb that goes with *he, she, it,* or any noun that can be replaced by *he, she,* or *it*. **Third person plural** refers to the form of the verb when the subject is *they* or any noun that can be replaced by *they*.

Here is the pattern **(conjugation)** for the verb *to walk* in the present tense:

First person singular:	**I walk**	First person plural:	**we walk**
Second person singular:	**you walk**	Second person plural:	**you walk**
Third person singular:	**he, she,** or **it walks**	Third person plural:	**they walk**

Notice the only weird form in the entire pattern is the **third person singular;** it always ends in *s*. It's interesting that *s* added to a noun makes the noun plural, but *s* added to a verb makes the verb third person singular.

Most languages have several different endings for verbs, depending on the subject's person and number. We're lucky that the present tense in English has just two separate verb endings, one for the third person singular and the other for all the other persons and numbers.

SOME TRICKY SITUATIONS IN SUBJECT-VERB AGREEMENT

A. Although the subject usually comes before the verb in English sentences, there are a couple of situations in which the verb comes before the subject. In order to know whether to use a singular or plural verb, you have to think through the sentence and determine what the subject is; then you can make the verb's number agree with the subject's number.

   1.   In sentences that begin with *there*, the subject comes after the verb:

There **is** a cookie for you on the kitchen table.
(The subject is *cookie*, so you need the singular verb *is*.)
There **are** lots of chocolate chips in it.
(The subject is *chips*, so you need the plural verb *are*.)
There **are** more cookies in the cupboard if you're still hungry.
(The subject is *cookies*, so you need the plural verb *are*.)

   2.   The verb (or part of it) comes before the subject in **questions:**

Is he the star of the Cosmic Clashes?
(The subject is *he*, so you need the singular verb *is*.)
Are Mongo and Chively going to the beach with us?
(The subject—*Mongo and Chively*—is plural, so you need the plural verb *are going*.)
Are there more cookies somewhere?
(The subject is *cookies*, so you need the plural verb *are*.)

Until you get the hang of identifying the subject in these situations, it's sometimes helpful to rearrange the words in your head, so the subject will come before the verb:

He is the star of the Cosmic Clashes. (OK—it's clear that the subject is *he* and the verb is *is*, so you can rearrange the order into question form again: *Is he the star of the Cosmic Clashes?*)
Mongo and Chively are going to the beach with us.
(subject = *Mongo and Chively*; verb = *are going*
question form = *Are Mongo and Chively going to the beach with us?*)
There are more cookies somewhere.
(subject = *cookies*; verb = *are*
question form = *Are there more cookies somewhere?*)

B. Many times, the noun that is right next to the verb isn't the simple subject:

One of my cousins **has** an airplane, a motorboat, and a turnip truck.
(The simple subject is *one*, so the verb must be third person singular even though the plural word *cousins* comes right before the verb.)

Please don't be confused by nouns or pronouns that follow *of*; they usually are not the simple subject, but merely parts of a prepositional phrase.

Small **copies** of that famous painting **are** on sale in the gift shop.
One of the copies **was** shredded by mistake yesterday.

C. Two or more singular subjects joined by *or* or *nor* take a *singular* verb; two or more singular subjects joined by *and* take a *plural* verb:

Neither Peony **nor** Mongo **likes** anchovies.
A salad **or** an apple **is** fine for lunch.
Peony **and** Mongo **hate** anchovies.
A salad **and** an apple **are** fine for dinner.

Exercise in Subject-Verb Agreement

Please underline the simple subject, and, from the choice in parentheses, circle the verb form that agrees in person and number with the subject.

1. Several members of your family (have   has) very long toes.
2. Many hands (make   makes) light work.
3. (Do   Does) the apple in your hand contain half a worm?
4. Mad dogs and Englishmen (go   goes) out in the noonday sun.
5. Why (are   is) there an evil grin on your face?
6. There (are   is) too many cooks flinging things into the broth.
7. I (like   likes) to wish on billions and billions of stars.
8. A pineapple or a mango (make   makes) a satisfying snack.

9. A pineapple and a mango (are   is) cooling in the refrigerator.

10. There (are   is) bells on the hill, but they (haven't   hasn't) rung yet.

11. Mongo (have   has) ring around the collar, but he (don't   doesn't) care.

12. One of my sisters (have   has) dentures, but she still (eats   eat) raspberries.

13. There (are   is) a big bug sitting on your head; there (are   is) all kinds of wildlife here in the suburbs.

14. The rain in Maine (fall   falls) plainly on the crane.

15. Several issues of *Today's Law Enforcement* (have   has) been stolen.

16. Neither my father nor my brother (wear   wears) a necktie every day.

17. Both my mother and my sister (like   likes) to listen to music by The Howling Skitters.

18. There (are   is) smoke billowing from the oven; (are   is) you testing the smoke alarm again?

19. One of the Three Stooges—Larry, Curly, or Mo—(are   is) appearing at our library next week.

20. The recipe and the mixer (are   is) waiting for you in the kitchen.

THE INFINITIVE

The **infinitive** gets its name because it doesn't have any boundaries of person, number, or tense. Just as people have first and last names, the infinitive is a verb's official name; the first name is always *to:*

to laugh	to love	to dream
to sing	to dance	to sigh
to celebrate	to mourn	to remember

When you speak or write of a verb as a word, use the infinitive form to avoid confusion, as some nouns and verb forms are identical—*dream, love, hug,* and *kiss,* for example. However, *to dream, to love, to hug,* and *to kiss* are clearly verbs.

The infinitive is handy because it gives us the root, or basic form of the verb; just remove the *to* from the infinitive, and you're left with the root, which is used to make other forms of the verb.

PRINCIPAL PARTS OF VERBS

Each verb has four principal parts: the **root form**, the **simple past**, the **past participle**, and the **present participle**.

The **PART**iciple is **PART** of a verb; a participle must be accompanied by an **auxiliary** (a "helping verb") in order to function as a verb.

The **present participle** always ends in *ing*. The present participle is helped by a form of *to be:*

I am walking.	I have been walking.
He is walking.	She has been walking.
They are walking.	I will be walking.

The past participle is helped by a form of *to have* (and sometimes by a form of *to be*):

I have walked.
He has walked.
I had walked.
I have been walked. (This is in the passive voice.)

Regular verbs are those whose simple past tense and past participle are formed merely by adding *d* or *ed*. The simple past form and the past participle of a regular verb are identical.

Root Form	Simple Past	Past Participle	Present Participle
walk	walked	walked	walking
love	loved	loved	loving

Regular verbs ending in *y* need special handling; if the letter right before the final *y* is a consonant (any letter except *a, e, i, o,* and *u,* which, you'll remember, are vowels), you change the *y* to *i* and add *ed* to form the simple past tense and the past participle:

Root Form	Simple Past	Past Participle	Present Participle
deny	denied	denied	denying
cry	cried	cried	crying
apply	applied	applied	applying

If, however, the letter right before the final *y* is a vowel, nothing special happens; you merely add *ed* to form the simple past tense and the past participle, just as you do with all the other regular verbs:

Root Form	Simple Past	Past Participle	Present Participle
pray	prayed	prayed	praying
display	displayed	displayed	displaying
relay	relayed	relayed	relaying

Irregular verbs are those whose simple past tense and past participle are not formed merely by adding *d* or *ed*. Worse yet, there is no single rule that governs these formations of irregular verbs, and they must be memorized through practice. Dictionaries usually give the principal parts of irregular verbs. If no principal parts are listed after a verb in the dictionary, it's safe to assume that the verb is regular (and troublefree).

Root Form	Simple Past	Past Participle	Present Participle
sing	sang	sung	singing
freeze	froze	frozen	freezing

PRINCIPAL PARTS OF SOME POPULAR IRREGULAR VERBS

Root Form	Simple Past	Past Participle (needs an auxiliary)	Present Participle (needs an auxiliary)
bear	bore	borne	bearing
beat	beat	beaten	beating
begin	began	begun	beginning
bend	bent	bent	bending
bind	bound	bound	binding
bite	bit	bitten	biting
bleed	bled	bled	bleeding
blow	blew	blown	blowing
break	broke	broken	breaking
breed	bred	bred	breeding
bring	brought	brought	bringing
build	built	built	building
burst	burst	burst	bursting
buy	bought	bought	buying
catch	caught	caught	catching
choose	chose	chosen	choosing
cling	clung	clung	clinging
come	came	come	coming
creep	crept	crept	creeping
deal	dealt	dealt	dealing
dig	dug	dug	digging
do	did	done	doing
draw	drew	drawn	drawing
drink	drank	drunk	drinking
drive	drove	driven	driving
dwell	dwelt	dwelt	dwelling
eat	ate	eaten	eating
fall	fell	fallen	falling
feed	fed	fed	feeding
feel	felt	felt	feeling
fight	fought	fought	fighting
find	found	found	finding

PRINCIPAL PARTS OF MORE IRREGULAR VERBS

Root Form	Simple Past	Past Participle (needs an auxiliary)	Present Participle (needs an auxiliary)
flee	fled	fled	fleeing
fling	flung	flung	flinging
fly	flew	flown	flying
forsake	forsook	forsaken	forsaking
freeze	froze	frozen	freezing
get	got	gotten	getting
give	gave	given	giving
go	went	gone	going
grind	ground	ground	grinding
grow	grew	grown	growing
hang[1]	hung	hung	hanging
have	had	had	having
hear	heard	heard	hearing
hide	hid	hidden	hiding
hit	hit	hit	hitting
hurt	hurt	hurt	hurting
keep	kept	kept	keeping
kneel	knelt	knelt	kneeling
know	knew	known	knowing
lay	laid	laid	laying
lead	led	led	leading
leave	left	left	leaving
lend	lent	lent	lending
lie	lay	lain	lying
light	lit	lit	lighting
lose	lost	lost	losing
make	made	made	making
mean	meant	meant	meaning
meet	met	met	meeting
pay	paid	paid	paying
put	put	put	putting
read	read[2]	read	reading
rend	rent	rent	rending
ride	rode	ridden	riding
ring	rang	rung	ringing

[1] When *to hang* means *to execute by hanging*, the past forms are regular: *hanged*.

[2] The past forms of *to read* are pronounced as if they were spelled *red*.

PRINCIPAL PARTS OF STILL MORE IRREGULAR VERBS

Root Form	Simple Past	Past Participle (needs an auxiliary)	Present Participle (needs an auxiliary)
rise	rose	risen	rising
run	ran	run	running
see	saw	seen	seeing
seek	sought	sought	seeking
sell	sold	sold	selling
send	sent	sent	sending
set	set	set	setting
shake	shook	shaken	shaking
shine[3]	shone	shone	shining
shoot	shot	shot	shooting
shrink	shrank	shrunk	shrinking
sing	sang	sung	singing
sink	sank	sunk	sinking
sit	sat	sat	sitting
slay	slew	slain	slaying
sleep	slept	slept	sleeping
slide	slid	slid	sliding
sling	slung	slung	slinging
slink	slunk	slunk	slinking
smite	smote	smitten	smiting
speak	spoke	spoken	speaking
spend	spent	spent	spending
spin	spun	spun	spinning
spring	sprang	sprung	springing
stand	stood	stood	standing
steal	stole	stolen	stealing
stick	stuck	stuck	sticking
sting	stung	stung	stinging
stink	stank	stunk	stinking
stride	strode	stridden	striding
strike	struck	struck	striking
string	strung	strung	stringing
strive	strove	striven	striving
swear	swore	sworn	swearing
sweep	swept	swept	sweeping
swim	swam	swum	swimming
swing	swung	swung	swinging

[3] *To shine* is irregular only when it means *to give off light;* when it means *to polish,* its forms are regular: *shined.*

PRINCIPAL PARTS OF EVEN MORE IRREGULAR VERBS

Root Form	Simple Past	Past Participle (needs an auxiliary)	Present Participle (needs an auxiliary)
take	took	taken	taking
teach	taught	taught	teaching
tear	tore	torn	tearing
tell	told	told	telling
think	thought	thought	thinking
throw	threw	thrown	throwing
tread	trod	trodden	treading
wear	wore	worn	wearing
weave	wove	woven	weaving
weep	wept	wept	weeping
win	won	won	winning
wind	wound	wound	winding
wring	wrung	wrung	wringing
write	wrote	written	writing

THE MOST WILDLY IRREGULAR VERB IN ENGLISH: *TO BE*

Root Form	Simple Past	Past Participle	Present Participle
am/is/are/be	was/were	been	being

Present Tense

First person singular:	**I am**	First person plural:	**we are**
Second person singular:	**you are**	Second person plural:	**you are**
Third person singular:	**he, she, it is**	Third person plural:	**they are**

Simple Past

First person singular:	**I was**	First person plural:	**we were**
Second person singular:	**you were**	Second person plural:	**you were**
Third person singular:	**he, she, it was**	Third person plural:	**they were**

Present Perfect

First person singular:	**I have been**	First person plural:	**we have been**
Second person singular:	**you have been**	Second person plural:	**you have been**
Third person singular:	**he, she, it has been**	Third person plural:	**they have been**

Future

First person singular:	**I will be**	First person plural:	**we will be**
Second person singular:	**you will be**	Second person plural:	**you will be**
Third person singular:	**he, she, it will be**	Third person plural:	**they will be**

AUXILIARY VERBS

Auxiliary (helping) verbs are wondrously useful; they help to form tenses, and they often give special emphasis and meaning to a verb.

Forms of *to be* and *to have* are the most common auxiliary verbs:

am	was
are	were
is	

I **am** serenading you.
She **is** serenading you.
They **are** serenading you.
He **was** serenading you.
We **were** serenading you.

have
has
had

I **have** serenaded you for weeks.
She **had** serenaded you before anyone else did.
They **have** serenaded you for days.
Even the parakeet **has** serenaded you.

Sometimes forms of *to be* and *to have* work together as auxiliary verbs:

I **have been** serenading you every day.

Here are some other handy auxiliary verbs:

do	could
does	would
did	should
may	can
might	will

Please **do** serenade me back, you magical creature.
You **did** serenade me after all, and my heart jumped up with joy.
Will you serenade me again?
May you serenade me forever!
You **can** serenade me any time you want to.
Rambo already **does** serenade me.
He **might** serenade Rambette, too.
He **could** serenade the birds right out of the trees.
I **would** serenade you even if you had earmuffs on.
I **should** serenade you at breakfast, but I'm losing my voice.

I **would** serenade you even if you had earmuffs on.
I **should** serenade you at breakfast, but I'm losing my voice.

OF

Did you notice that *of* didn't appear in the list of auxiliary verbs? *Of* isn't even a verb (you know that it's a preposition), so the poor old thing couldn't *possibly* function as an auxiliary verb. You have probably seen sentences like this, though:

I could of eaten the whole package of cream horns by myself.
You should of called when you knew you were going to be late.

Needless to say, these constructions are wrong, but it's fun to try to puzzle out how *of* got hauled into them as an auxiliary verb. Perhaps someone once *heard* a person say

I **could've** eaten the whole package of cream horns by myself.

or

You **should've** called when you knew you were going to be late.

The contractions *could've* for *could have* and *should've* for *should have* are perfectly acceptable, but you can see how someone might have heard these as *could of* and *should of*; say *could've* and *should've* to yourself. Now that you understand this mistake, you will never be tempted to write *of* instead of *have* after *could, would, should,* and *might.*

TENSE

I cleaned the carburetor tomorrow.
I will clean the gas tank yesterday.

Sentences like these make your teeth hurt because you can tell instantly that something is very wrong; this shows that you already know something about verb tenses. The **tense** of a verb refers to time, and you probably recognized that the verbs in the sentences above already had their own time built in. The *ed* in *cleaned* told you that the cleaning is finished, and that's why the *tomorrow* in the same sentence gave you dental twinges. Also, *will clean* points toward the future, and it certainly seems strange with *yesterday.*

I cleaned the carburetor yesterday.
I will clean the gas tank tomorrow.

PRESENT TENSE

The **present tense** of a verb indicates that the action or state described is taking place now or that it takes place regularly.

You are the happiest person in the state.
Rambo likes tanks this year.
She jumps on the trampoline at dawn.

SIMPLE PAST TENSE

A verb in the **simple past tense** indicates that the action or state described both began and ended in the past.

You were the happiest person in the state.
Rambo liked Jeeps last year.
She jumped on the trampoline at dawn.

To form the simple past tense of a regular verb, merely add *d* to the root if the verb ends in *e*; add *ed* to the root if the verb doesn't end in *e*.
  Here is the conjugation of the verb *to walk* in the simple past tense:

First person singular:	**I walked**	First person plural:	**we walked**
Second person singular:	**you walked**	Second person plural:	**you walked**
Third person singular:	**he, she,** or **it walked**	Third person plural:	**they walked**

Isn't that gloriously easy? Since all the forms in the simple past tense are the same, with no special form for the third person singular to worry about, there is never any problem with subject-verb agreement in the simple past tense.

FUTURE TENSE

The **future tense** indicates a future action or state.

I will celebrate tomorrow.
My team will win the trophy next year.

To form the future tense, merely insert *will* before the root form of the verb. All the forms are the same, so there are no special subject-verb agreement problems.
  Here's the conjugation of *to walk* in the future tense:

First person singular:	**I will walk**	First person plural:	**we will walk**
Second person singular:	**you will walk**	Second person plural:	**you will walk**
Third person singular:	**he, she,** or **it will walk**	Third person plural:	**they will walk**

Tense Exercise

Beside the number, please name the tense (present, simple past, or future) of the *italicized* verb.

Example:

Simple Past   They *giggled* when I stood up to speak.

_____   1. They *will regret* their behavior.

_____   2. I *will* never *smile* at them again.

_____ 3. Mongo *holds* his breath during scary videos.

_____ 4. Peony *jumped* into the pool with her fuchsia boots on.

_____ 5. She *does* that at least once a week.

_____ 6. Elmo *attended* the Save the Wombat Rally last night.

_____ 7. He *will attend* the rally in Toronto next week.

_____ 8. He *attends* every wombat rally he can find.

_____ 9. Rats on a twig! I *burned* the popcorn again!

_____ 10. The flame on this acetylene torch *is* far too hot.

_____ 11. If you *will get* some more popcorn. I'll give it another shot.

_____ 12. I *require* popcorn and papaya juice for complete happiness.

_____ 13. Your toucan *will molt* next month.

_____ 14. It *molted* all over the house last year.

_____ 15. I *cleaned* feathers out of the toaster for weeks.

Conjugation Exercise

In the following spaces, please supply the proper forms for the verb *to miss* in the present tense. (Handy hint: if the root already ends in s, you'll need to add *es* to form the third person singular; this adds another syllable and makes the word pronounceable.)

First person singular: _____   First person plural: _____

Second person singular: _____   Second person plural: _____

Third person singular: _____   Third person plural: _____

In the following spaces, supply the proper forms for the verb *to bathe* in the simple past tense (add *d* to the **root**).

First person singular: _____   First person plural: _____

Second person singular: _____   Second person plural: _____

Third person singular: _____   Third person plural: _____

In the following spaces, supply the proper forms for the verb *to smile* in the future tense (*will* + **root**):

First person singular: _____   First person plural: _____

Second person singular: _____   Second person plural: _____

Third person singular: _____   Third person plural: _____

Another Verb Exercise

1. Please write five sentences about Peony McAllister; put all your verbs in the present tense.

_____

_____

_____

_____

_____

2. Write a sentence containing *three* verbs in the simple past tense.

_____

3. Write a sentence containing *three* verbs in the present perfect tense.

_____

4. Write a sentence containing *three* verbs in the future tense.

_____

5. If the regular verb *to zork* existed, how would you conjugate it in the present tense?

First person singular: _____   First person plural: _____

Second person singular: _____   Second person plural: _____

Third person singular: _____   Third person plural: _____

6. Now conjugate *to zork* (what do you suppose it would mean?) in the simple past tense.

First person singular: _____   First person plural: _____

Second person singular: _____   Second person plural: _____

Third person singular: _____   Third person plural: _____

7. Now conjugate *to zork* in the future tense.

First person singular: _____   First person plural: _____

Second person singular: _____   Second person plural: _____

Third person singular: _____   Third person plural: _____

A FEW MORE TENSES: PERFECTS

Don't let the name of this group of tenses worry you—"perfect" doesn't mean absolutely without flaw here—it's just a user-friendly grammatical label. The perfect tenses indicate action or states that have already been completed. All three of the perfect tenses use the **past participle.**

Present Perfect

The **present perfect tense** specifies an action or state that began and ended in the past or that began in the past and continues into the present. The present perfect tense is formed by adding *has* or *have* (depending on the subject's number) to the **past participle.** The past participle of a regular verb looks exactly like the simple past form, just add *d* or *ed* to the root.

The past participles of irregular verbs are sometimes wild and crazy—feel free to consult the "Principal Parts of Some Popular Irregular Verbs" section (pages 106–109) until you're thoroughly familiar with the forms.

They **have** already **done** their homework for tomorrow.
You **have smelled** like wintergreen all day.
Mongo **has left** the dishes in the sink again.

Conjugation Exercise

Please supply the proper forms for the verb *to smile* in the present perfect tense (*have* or *has* + the **past participle**):

First person singular: _____   First person plural: _____

Second person singular: _____   Second person plural: _____

Third person singular: _____   Third person plural: _____

Some Words of Caution

Beware of letting the past participle of an irregular verb try to do the work of a verb without the participle having an auxiliary to help it:

I seen Captain Kangaroo at the mall.
She done three loads of laundry in ten minutes.

Beware, too, of tossing an auxiliary in front of a plain old simple past irregular verb (the simple past doesn't need any help to do what it has to do):

I have saw Captain Kangaroo at the mall.
She has did three loads of laundry in ten minutes.

You now know why you should say:

I have seen Captain Kangaroo at the mall.
I saw Captain Kangaroo at the mall.
She has done three loads of laundry in ten minutes.
She did three loads of laundry in ten minutes.

Past Perfect

The **past perfect tense** (sometimes called the **pluperfect,** which is kind of fun to say) indicates that the action or state began in the past and ended at some later time in the past. It is formed by using *had* + the **past participle.** (Any other verb in the sentence must be in the more recent past than the past perfect.)

Peony remembered that she **had heard** that lecture before.
I **had** already **finished** breakfast when you called.

Exercise

Please write a sentence containing the verb *to smile* in the past perfect tense.

_____

Future Perfect

You don't hear the future perfect tense very often these days, but there's no harm in knowing about it. The **future perfect tense** indicates a future action or state that will be completed at a specific time. It is formed by using *will have* + the **past participle.**

Next Monday, I **will have spent** a whole week without television.
By this time next month, you **will have walked** across the state.

Exercise

Write a sentence containing the verb *to smile* in the future perfect tense.

_____

Another Small Exercise

Please conjugate the imaginary regular verb *to fiffle* in the present perfect tense.

First person singular: _____   First person plural: _____

Second person singular: _____   Second person plural: _____

Third person singular: _____   Third person plural: _____

Conjugate *to fiffle* in the past perfect tense.

First person singular: _____   First person plural: _____

Second person singular: _____   Second person plural: _____

Third person singular: _____   Third person plural: _____

JUST A FEW MORE TENSES: PROGRESSIVES

Here's a useful bit of information: all of the progressive tenses use the present participle (the *ing* one). Stay tuned!

Present Progressive

The **present progressive tense** indicates that the action or state is in progress right now; it is formed with *am, is,* or *are* + the **present participle** (the *ing* one).

I **am racing.**
He **is cheering** for me.
She **is waving** the flag.
The spectators **are roaring** their encouragement.
I **am being** applauded.

You may have noticed that people often use the present progressive tense for something that will take place in the future, which is OK in all but the most formal circumstances.

I am going to the store tomorrow.
Are you entering the tambourine competition next week?

Exercise

Write a sentence containing the verb *to laugh* in the present progressive tense.

Past Progressive

The **past progressive tense** indicates that the action or state was in progress in the past; it is formed with *was* or *were* + the **present participle** (the *ing* one).

She **was leaving** for the bus station.
He **was asking** her not to go.
They **were planning** to meet in Poughkeepsie.
We **were dying** to know the details.

Exercise

Write a sentence containing the verb *to laugh* in the past progressive tense.

_____

Future Progressive

The **future progressive tense** indicates that the action or state will be in progress in the future; it is formed with *will be* + the **present participle** (the *ing* one).

I **will be singing.**
You **will be playing** the guitar.
He **will be covering** his ears.
We **will be having** fun.
They **will be dancing** in the streets.

Exercise

Please write a sentence containing the verb *to laugh* in the future progressive tense.

_____

Present Perfect Progressive

The **present perfect progressive tense** indicates that the action or state started in the past and is still in progress; it is formed with *has been* or *have been* + the **present participle** (the *ing* one).

I **have been reading** since dawn.
You **have been sleeping** like a stone.
He **has been working** overtime all week.
We **have been dancing** at the Aloha Saloon on weekends.
They **have been singing** in the choir for forty-six years.

Exercise

Write a sentence containing the verb *to laugh* in the present perfect progressive tense.

_____

There is a **future perfect progressive tense,** too: Cinderella *will have been cleaning* the dungeon for three hours when Prince gets there. Here's the **past perfect progressive:** Before I learned how to operate a flashlight, I *had been bumping* into walls a lot.

One More Conjugation Exercise

Please conjugate the imaginary regular verb *to greble* in the present progressive tense.

First person singular: _____   First person plural: _____

Second person singular: _____   Second person plural: _____

Third person singular: _____   Third person plural: _____

Now conjugate *to greble* in the present perfect progressive tense.

First person singular: _____   First person plural: _____

Second person singular: _____   Second person plural: _____

Third person singular: _____   Third person plural: _____

Conjugate *to greble* in the future progressive tense.

First person singular: _____   First person plural: _____

Second person singular: _____   Second person plural: _____

Third person singular: _____   Third person plural: _____

HANDY HINTS FOR RECOGNIZING TENSES

The plain old **present tense** has just one word in the verb (except in the passive voice, which we'll get to soon).

The plain old **simple past** has just one word in the verb (except in the passive voice—stay tuned).

Any tense with the word **perfect** in its name has to have *has, have,* or *had* in it, along with the past participle. There will be at least two words in the verb.

Any tense with the word **progressive** in its name uses the present participle (the *ing* one) and at least one auxiliary verb. There will be at least two words in the verb.

Any tense with the word **future** in its name has to start with the word *will.* There will be at least two words in the verb.

More Tense Exercises

A. Please change the *italicized* verbs in these sentences to the present progressive tense.

1. We *will pick* buttercups behind the barn.
2. She *sings* sad songs in the moonlight.
3. Jaws, my pet wombat, *ate* my license plate.

4. Rambette *will toss* grenades at the termites.
5. Grandma *bought* a plastic dress.

B. Change the italicized verbs in these sentences to the present perfect tense.

1. I *am losing* my patience with this wretched computer.
2. *Are* you *going* to the Cosmic Clashes concert?
3. Many *will volunteer*, but few *are* reliable.
4. I *ate* three packages of cream horns for breakfast.
5. *Are* you *living* here?

C. Change the italicized verbs in these sentences to the past perfect tense.

1. Someone *left* the cake out in the rain.
2. London Bridge *is falling* down; we can hardly expect it to fall up.
3. You *have used* the last little bit of toothpaste.
4. She *will eat* only bee brains and ant livers for a whole week.
5. The mean crocodile completely *demolished* Tarzan's waterwings.

D. Change the italicized verbs in these sentences to the past progressive tense.

1. Mongo *swept* the dust bunnies into the mailbox.
2. I *looked* for a silver lining in the cloud.
3. Peony *has ridden* her motorcycle all over the Southwest.
4. *Will* you *buy* some chokecherry cookies at the bakery?
5. The gerbils *escaped* through a hole in the ceiling.

FUN WITH VERBS

If the *italicized* verb is incorrect, please replace it with the correct form (feel free to refer to the lists of irregular verbs); if the form of the verb is correct, write *OK* above it.

Example:

She *throwed* all of our yogurt down the sink, so we *left*.

1. Fedonia *shined* her shoes and *done* her nails before breakfast.
2. Nobody *knowed* the truffles the chef *has saw*.
3. They *seen* the roadblock, but they *was going* too fast to stop.
4. The woodchucks *chucked* wood until they *busted*.

5. Larry and Darryl *have brung* their lunch in a burlap sack again; they *brang* critter-ear sandwiches yesterday.

6. Mongo *has* finally *did* what I told him to do; he *seen* a dentist.

7. He *might of thunk* that I wouldn't notice, but he *was* wrong.

8. Sadie *sayed* that she *has saw* everything in the mall and *has tryed* most of it on.

9. Elmo *has ridden* the bumper cars all day and *hasn't* once *hurt* himself.

10. Mongo *has took* the last piece of pizza; he *wrote* a note and *leaved* it in the box.

11. Daddy, I *bringed* a frog home from the pond and *throwed* him in the washing machine.

12. Her paper dress *shrunk* in the rain, and Peony *weeped* with embarrassment.

13. Yesterday, Grandma *ask* Leroy to behave himself, but he *slided* down the banister and *broke* his arm.

14. The crows *sung*, my boat *sunk*, and my pet python accidentally *hanged* himself in the apple tree; yesterday *stunk*!

15. Tarzan *swung* on vines, *swam* in the crocodile-infested river, *sped* over the mountain, and *bought* a Big Mac for Jane.

TENSE SHIFTS

Try not to shift tenses in mid-sentence unless there's a good reason. An unnecessary shift in tenses will confuse your readers, and your point won't get across to them.

She **was** relieved when the professor **hands** the tests back.

This would make a reader think that you got lost in your own sentence; the first verb is in the simple past tense, but the second one is in the present tense. The remedy is simple:

She **was** relieved when the professor **handed** the tests back.

or

She **is** relieved when the professor **hands** the tests back.

Something like this is OK, though:

She **had** already **chained** the burglar to the tree by the time help **arrived.**

Remember that when there is a past tense in a sentence, other verbs have to be in the more recent past.

Exercise

Look carefully at the verbs in the following sentences. If there are confusing shifts in tense, please fix them. If, however, the tenses are all right, write *OK* beside the sentence.

1. Elmo had walked two miles before he realized that he was barefoot.
2. Whenever the teacher talks to them, their faces will be squinching up.
3. I saw a tall, dark, handsome pirate in the pond, so I faint.
4. Mongo rents a video every day because he likes movies a lot.
5. King Kong started to think sweet thoughts, so he stops eating honey.

MOODS OF VERBS

Verbs have three moods, and you are already familiar with at least two of them.
The **indicative mood** indicates a statement of fact or asks a question.

Dr. Doom's midnight television program is very popular.
Is he a real person?

The **imperative mood** expresses a command.

Do come in!
Get out of town!
Please leave me alone!

The **subjunctive mood** expresses a wish, a possibility, a doubt, or something contrary to fact. You have probably heard the subjunctive mood every day.

If I were you, I'd count my blessings.

You may have wondered why the expression is "if I *were* you" instead of "if I *was* you." The rules of subject-verb agreement, after all, insist that the simple past tense of *to be* in the first person singular is *was*.
Look carefully at the sentence, though; it is expressing something that is contrary to fact: I am *not* you and never can be. Therefore, the sentence uses the subjunctive form *were* to convey that extra thought.
In your reading, you might see other subjunctive expressions:

Let there **be** music.
Would that I **were** with you in Tahiti!
Lest he **get** conceited, let's ease up on the compliments.

The contrary-to-fact subjunctive is by far the most common, though, so be on the lookout for situations that require it.

She has fallen arches, but if she **were** an astronaut, she'd suffer from missile toe.
If I **were** Queen of the Universe, I'd abolish tofu.

VOICE

Verbs have two voices, **active** and **passive.** A verb is in the **active voice** when the subject is performing the action:

The princess **kissed** the frog.

Kissed is in the **active voice** here; the subject of the sentence is *princess,* and she is doing the kissing.

A verb is in the **passive voice** when the subject is receiving the action:

The frog **was kissed** by the princess.

Was kissed is in the passive voice here; the subject of the sentence is *frog,* and it is being *acted upon.* (The performer of the action is tucked away in a prepositional phrase: *by the princess.*)

The **passive voice** is formed by using the *past participle* of the verb with some form of the verb *to be.*

The frog **is kissed** by the princess every day.
The frog **is being kissed** by the princess at this very moment.
The frog **was kissed** by the princess yesterday.
The frog **was being kissed** by the princess when the tornado struck.
The frog **will be kissed** by the windblown princess tomorrow.
The frog **has been kissed** by the princess approximately 5,924 times.
The frog **had been kissed** by the queen before the princess arrived.
By next Thursday, the frog **will have been kissed** to death by the princess.

As you can see, a verb in the passive voice always has at least two words in it.

Exercise in Recognizing Verbs in the Passive Voice

Please underline the subject in each of the following sentences; then, beside the number, write *active* if the subject is doing the acting or *passive* if the subject is receiving the action.

Examples:

Passive   The anthill was examined by the little boy.
active   The little boy examined the anthill.

_____ 1. The squid stew was spoiled by too many cooks.

_____ 2. Too many cooks spoiled the squid stew.

_____ 3. My neighbor's house was demolished by termites.

_____ 4. Termites demolished my neighbor's house.

_____ 5. He is being sheltered by the Red Cross.

_____ 6. The Red Cross is sheltering him.

_____ 7. The falling chandelier interrupted the party.

_____ 8. The party was interrupted by the falling chandelier.

_____ 9. Rambo was frightened by the tiny mouse.

_____ 10. The tiny mouse frightened Rambo.

_____ 11. A concert was given by The Howling Skitters.

_____ 12. The Howling Skitters gave a concert.

_____ 13. Mongo put the check in the mail.

_____ 14. The check was put in the mail by Mongo.

_____ 15. I was blasted out of bed by the alarm clock.

_____ 16. The alarm clock blasted me out of bed.

_____ 17. The lost hiker was finally found by the Royal Canadian Mounted Police.

_____ 18. The Royal Canadian Mounted Police finally found the lost hiker.

_____ 19. Grandpa was lured into the kitchen by the aroma of baking cookies.

_____ 20. The aroma of baking cookies lured Grandpa into the kitchen.

MORE ABOUT VERBS IN THE PASSIVE VOICE

Now that you know how to recognize verbs in the passive voice, try to be careful with them. Passive verbs tend to weaken a sentence; moreover, passive verbs leave some very important questions unanswered.

It was reported that the treasury secretary can't count higher than five.

Who reported this startling news? The sentence doesn't tell us, and knowing the reporter's identity and credibility is important.
    If the treasury secretary's mother reported it, it may be true.
    If a bitter enemy of the treasury secretary reported it, there is some doubt.
    If a supermarket scandal sheet reported it, it's probably false.
    Getting rid of the passive verb can clear up a lot of murkiness.

The *Grocery Gazette* reported that the treasury secretary can't count higher than five.

Here's another miracle of vagueness.

It has been learned that the world will end tomorrow.

What is the subject? *It.* What does *it* mean? *It* = that the world will end tomorrow. Who learned that the world will end tomorrow? The sentence doesn't tell us, and this information could make a lot of difference about how we receive the news.

If a Pentagon spokesman told Civil Defense Headquarters, it may be true.

If someone read it on a bubblegum wrapper, there's probably not much to worry about.

Passive verbs are certainly not forbidden, but you should have a healthy respect for them and use them only with great care and forethought.

Exercise in Changing Passive Verbs to Active Verbs

Look carefully at this sentence containing a passive verb:

subject passive verb prepositional phrase
My cat was irritated by your canary.

To find out what the subject of your new sentence (with an active verb) will be, ask yourself who is performing the action in the passive sentence. Usually, the actor is tucked away in a prepositional phrase beginning with *by*.

Once you have located the actor, it is easy to change the passive *was irritated* to the very active *irritated*:

subject   active verb direct object
Your canary irritated   my cat.

Following the preceding steps, change the verbs in the following sentences from the passive voice to the active voice. Circle the actor in each sentence.

1. The sheep were lost by absent-minded Bo Peep.
2. The teacher was encouraged by the students' smiles.
3. My tent was blown away by the wind.
4. Chuckles the Clown was hired by the circus.
5. The frog was changed into a handsome accountant by the princess's kiss.
6. The pants were made too long by the tailor.
7. The bananas were stolen by the escaped chimpanzee.
8. The cat was killed by curiosity.
9. The dungeon was decorated by Cinderella.
10. The dancer's wooden shoes were eaten by termites.

ACTIVE-PASSIVE MIXTURES

It's a good idea to avoid mixing active and passive verbs in the same sentence unless there's a good reason.

We **went** to the concert, and it **was enjoyed** by all of us.

Such a mixture makes a sentence unnecessarily bulky, and your readers have to work hard to figure out what you're saying.

We **went** to the concert, and all of us **enjoyed** it.

Exercise

Change any passive verbs you find in the sentences below to active; then make any other appropriate changes necessary for a smooth, clear sentence.

1. Your bill was received by her, and she threw it into the well.
2. Plastic Man was melted by the witch, and she turned him into a credit card.
3. The opera star sang the difficult song, and then she gargled with root beer.
4. The table was set by Grandma while Grandpa mashed the turnips.
5. The chickens were stolen by the hungry pirate, and we suspected foul play.

LIVELY VERBS FOR LIVELY WRITING

We have seen that active verbs are stronger than passive verbs, but even some active verbs just lie there and refuse to do anything zingy. The verb *to say* is popular, but it certainly isn't action-packed.

"Oh," she said.

This has all the power and zing of old, cold oatmeal. There are dozens of verbs that can make this sentence vivid and exciting:

"Oh," she **whispered.**
"Oh," she **moaned.**
"Oh," she **giggled.**
"Oh," she **muttered.**
"Oh," she **yodeled.**
"Oh," she **wailed.**
"Oh," she **squealed.**
"Oh," she **roared.**
"Oh," she **groaned.**
"Oh," she **chirped.**
"Oh," she **sang.**
"Oh," she **squeaked.**
"Oh," she **whined.**
"Oh," she **sobbed.**
"Oh," she **croaked.**
"Oh," she **screamed.**
"Oh," she **crooned.**
"Oh," she **cackled.**
"Oh," she **chuckled.**

"Oh," she **sputtered.**
"Oh," she **gasped.**
"Oh," she **shrieked.**
"Oh," she **bubbled.**
"Oh," she **babbled.**
"Oh," she **sneered.**
"Oh," she **wheezed.**
"Oh," she **snorted.**
"Oh," she **snarled.**
"Oh," she **growled.**
"Oh," she **grumbled.**
"Oh," she **grunted.**
"Oh," she **yelped.**
"Oh," she **squawked.**
"Oh," she **yawned.**
"Oh," she **crowed.**
"Oh," she **trilled.**
"Oh," she **bellowed.**
"Oh," she **whinnied.**
"Oh," she **bleated.**
"Oh," she **yipped.**
"Oh," she **sighed.**
"Oh," she **shouted.**
"Oh," she **gurgled.**
"Oh," she **whimpered.**
"Oh," she **simpered.**
"Oh," she **whooped.**
"Oh," she **howled.**
"Oh," she **yowled.**

Instead of relying on *to say*, *to be*, or *to go*, search your vocabulary for a verb that tells the reader how the subject sounds, looks, or acts. Your readers will bless you for keeping them awake and interested, and you'll discover how much fun writing can be.

Exercise

Replace the italicized verbs with as many lively ones as you can—go wild!

1. Hungry tigers *were* around our tent.
2. The dragon *went* to the castle.

TRANSITIVE AND INTRANSITIVE VERBS

A verb is **transitive** when it needs a **direct object** (a noun or pronoun that receives the action of the verb) to complete its meaning.

The finicky canary threw its breakfast at the wall.

Breakfast receives the action of the verb *threw*; therefore, *threw* is a **transitive verb,** and *breakfast* is the **direct object.**

An easy way to look for the direct object is to ask *whom* or *what* after the verb:

Threw whom or what? Breakfast.

An answer to the *whom* or *what* question will always give you the direct object.

An **intransitive verb** doesn't need a direct object to complete its meaning.

Donner and Blitzen slept from Christmas till Labor Day.
Slept whom or what?

There is no answer to the *whom* or *what* question (from Christmas till Labor Day tells *when*, and that's not what we're asking); *slept* is **intransitive.**

The presence of a direct object determines whether a verb is transitive or intransitive: in

Tootles sang sad songs in the moonlight.

sang is transitive because there's a direct object, *sad songs*. However, in

Tootles sang in the moonlight.

sang is intransitive because there is no direct object. In case you have ever wondered what "intr. v." and "tr. v." mean after a word in the dictionary, your wondering days are over: they are abbreviations for "intransitive verb" and "transitive verb." By the way, only **transitive verbs** can be put into the **passive voice,** when what is receiving the action (the direct object) becomes the subject.

Exercise

Beside the number, please write *t* if the verb is transitive and *i* if the verb is intransitive. Circle the direct object of transitive verbs.

Examples:

    t   The quarterback *hugged* the football.

    i   The football *exploded*.

_____ 1. Larry and Darryl *have been hunting* all morning

_____ 2. They finally *trapped* a critter.

_____ 3. The frightened critter *trembled*.

_____ 4. Larry *ate* a critter sandwich.

_____ 5. Larry *got* very *sick*.

_____ 6. I *held* Larry's hand.

_____   7. He *moaned* for three days.

_____   8. He *made* a solemn vow.

_____   9. He *will* never *touch* another critter sandwich.

_____ 10. We all *cheered.*

SIX VERY CONFUSING VERBS

Knowing the difference between transitive and intransitive verbs will help you with six very confusing verbs: *to sit* and *to set, to lie* and *to lay,* and *to rise* and *to raise.*
To set, to lay, and to raise are transitive verbs; they *must* have a direct object:

Set my present on the throne, please.
(*Set* whom or what? *My present.*)
Lay your throbbing head on my shoulder.
Lay whom or what? *Your throbbing head.*)
Raise your hand if you need help.
(*Raise* whom or what? *Your hand.*)

To sit, to lie, and to rise are intransitive; they don't need a direct object.

My present **sits** on the throne and waits.
(*Sits* whom or what? There is no direct object.)
Your throbbing head **is lying** on my shoulder.
(*Is* lying whom or what? There is no direct object.)
Your hand seems **to rise** all by itself.
(*To rise* whom or what? There is no direct object.)

To sit/To set

Root Form	Simple Past	Past Participle	Present Participle
sit	sat	sat	sitting
set	set	set	setting

To sit means merely to place one's posterior upon a surface:

Sit on your suitcase until the taxi arrives.

To sit never takes a direct object.
One of the meanings of *to set* is to place (something).

Set the cauldron on the back burner until Halloween.

When it is used to mean *to place, to set* must have a direct object. (When *to set* appears in connection with the sun, hens, cement, or Jell-O, it doesn't mean *to place,* so there's nothing to worry about.)

Exercise

Circle the correct verb in parentheses in these sentences.

1. Peony (sets   sits) beside the pool in her snowsuit, waiting for July.
2. Mongo (set   sat) in the corner and hummed ominously.
3. Why did you (set   sit) the muddy tractor tire on the kitchen table?
4. (Sit   Set) your books down and come have some hot cocoa.
5. I have (sat   set) in this airport for eleven hours, and my seat has turned to stone.

To lie/To lay

Root Form	Simple Past	Past Participle	Present Participle
lie	lay	lain	lying
lay	laid	laid	laying

There are two verbs *to lie:* one of them means merely *to tell a falsehood,* and it's a regular verb that never gives anyone any grief at all (except the people on the receiving end of the falsehood).

The verb *to lie* that gives people trouble means *to recline:*

I like **to lie** on the raft in the middle of the lake.

To lie never takes a direct object.

To lay is another way of saying *to place* (something). It means the same as *to set* and *to place*, and it is as transitive as a verb can get; it *must* have a direct object.

Lay down your slingshot, Cactus Pete, and come out with your hands up.

The simple past of *to lie* is very tricky because it doesn't even look like a past tense. Read the following examples quietly to yourself to get the feel of the word in your mouth:

Last week I **lay** in the meadow and saw pictures in the clouds.
Amyliz **lay** in bed and watched television all day yesterday.

Notice that the simple past form of *to lie* is *lay* and that the present tense of *to lay* is *lay*. That's why knowing these two verbs backwards and forwards is important; otherwise, things get hopelessly muddled.

Exercise

Circle the correct verb in parentheses in these sentences:

1. Peony (lies   lays) beside the pool in her snowsuit, waiting for July.
2. Mongo (lay   laid) in the corner and hummed ominously.

3. Why did you (lie   lay) that muddy tractor tire on the kitchen table?

4. (Lie   Lay) your books down and come have some hot cocoa.

5. I have (lain   laid) on this waterbed for an hour, and I'm seasick.

To rise/To raise

Root Form	Simple Past	Past Participle	Present Participle
rise	rose	risen	rising
raise	raised	raised	raising

To rise means merely *to get up* (the opposite of *to sit* and *to lie*):

The judge is skipping into the courtroom, so please **rise.**

To rise never takes a direct object.
    To raise means *to make something higher* (the opposite of *to set* and *to lay*):

We used telephone books **to raise** Tiny Alice's seat, so she could reach the table.

To raise must have a direct object.

Exercise

Circle the correct verb in parentheses in these sentences:

1. The men (rose   raised) their hats when they met Grandma on the street.

2. The moon (will raise   will rise) during the hayride.

3. With one hand, the burly mechanic (rose   raised) the subcompact car.

4. The champion (rose   raised) to receive the trophy.

5. When she sat on a cactus by mistake, Gypsy (raised   rose) suddenly.

Exercise in Confusing Verbs

From the choice in parentheses, circle the correct verb.

1. Your pet alligator is (sitting   setting) on my stomach.

2. Never (rise   raise) your voice in the library.

3. Mongo was sore after aerobics; he couldn't (rise   raise) his arms above his knees.

4. He was in such pain that he couldn't (raise   rise) from his bed.

5. My shopping list has disappeared, and I know I (lay   laid) it on the table just a minute ago.

6. Lazlo (lay   laid) in the hammock yesterday and never got around to mowing the lawn.

7. The mission will be almost impossible, but I know that you can (rise   raise) to the challenge.

8. The shark (raised   rose) to the surface to see who was for lunch.

9. If you're going to (lie   lay) down on the clean bedspread, please remove your wet raincoat.

10. Babe (lay   laid) her pistol down and took up golf.

11. Sleeping Beauty has (lain   laid) in her bed of rose petals for a century.

12. I had just (laid   lain) my head on my pillow when the doorbell rang.

13. The submarine captain (raised   rose) the periscope and saw an octopus's eye staring back at her.

14. The boss (lay   laid) the groundwork for my promotion last week.

15. Please don't (sit   set) the box of gold on Grandma's fragile table.

LINKING VERBS

Action versus **state of being** is yet another way to classify verbs.

The verb *to be* (in all its forms) is the only verb in English that is always a state-of-being verb and never an action verb. A state-of-being verb is also known as a **linking verb** because it links the subject to an adjective or to a noun.

A few verbs are sometimes action verbs and sometimes linking verbs:

To taste

This banana split **tastes** wonderful. (*tastes* is a **linking verb** here)
He reluctantly **tasted** the batwing stew. (*tasted* is an **action verb** here)

To sound

The Howling Skitters **sound** terrific tonight. **(linking)**
I **will sound** the alarm when the Martians land. **(action)**

To smell

Mongo's garlic air-freshener **smells** awful. **(linking)**
I **smelled** a rat when the cheese disappeared. **(action)**

To feel

I **feel** queasy after eating the marshmallow pizza. **(linking)**
The princess **felt** the small pea under fifteen mattresses. **(action)**

To look

Those ballet slippers **look** weird on Rambo's feet. **(linking)**
I **looked** carefully for route signs, but there weren't any. **(action)**

To become

> After not hearing from him for three weeks, I **became** alarmed. **(linking)**
> Moonlight **becomes** you; it goes with your hair. **(action)**

To remain

> The dieters **have remained** cheerful through thick and thin. **(linking)**
> Stubbornly, Bull **remained** until the hostess started yawning. **(action)**

Adverbs describe action verbs:

> Ollie oils his owl often.
> Ralph romps through the river recklessly.
> Ivan inspects his income infrequently.

Nothing describes linking verbs; they merely serve as a bridge between the subject and more information about the subject:

> This milkshake tastes sour.
> I am restless.
> My neighbor is a veteran.
> The soprano sounds flat.
> You look wonderful in a leather jacket.
> Chauncy remains my dearest friend.

MORE ABOUT LINKING VERBS

People who have not learned the distinction between action verbs and linking verbs sometimes are guilty of a grammatical fault called **hypercorrection;** they realize that they have used a verb, and they think that they must then automatically use an adverb with it. They say things like:

> I feel badly about my alligator's accident.
> That mink necktie looks well on you.

It's important to remember that linking verbs do not take adverbs. For instance, an adverb that tries to go with any form of the verb *to be* is doomed:

> I am happily.
> He was sadly.
> They will be hungrily.

Adverbs that accompany the other linking verbs sound all right until you figure out what is really going on in the sentence.

> I feel badly about my alligator's accident.
> (Since adverbs may accompany only action verbs, we must conclude that *to feel* is an

action verb here. This sentence therefore says that my fingers aren't working as they should, so I feel badly.)

The sentence should say

I feel bad about my alligator's accident.

Now you know why this sentence is wrong:

That mink necktie looks well on you.
(*Well* is an adjective only when it means *healthy*, which wouldn't make any sense here. As an adverb, it forces us to interpret *to look* as an action verb; this has to mean that the mink necktie has 20-20 vision.)

The sentence should say

That mink necktie looks good on you.

Here's another one:

That dead mackerel smells terribly.
(The adverb forces us to interpret *to smell* as an action verb, which makes the sentence say that there is something wrong with the poor fish's nose—as indeed there might be; it's dead, after all.)

The sentence should say

That dead mackerel smells terrible.

Exercise in Linking Verbs

Think very carefully about the verbs in the following sentences, and then circle the word from the choice in parentheses that will make the sentence correct and sensible. Mark each verb that appears before the parentheses *A* for "action" or *L* for "linking." Take your time!

1. Mongo's new aftershave lotion smells (terrible   terribly).
2. This chicken gizzard tastes (bitter   bitterly).
3. These fuchsia boots feel (comfortable   comfortably) on my feet.
4. You look (well   good) in toreador pants.
5. I am (hungry   hungrily), (thirsty   thirstily), and (sore   sorely).
6. Rambo felt (bad   badly) when the inspector fell into the boobytrap.
7. This squid sherbet with hazelnut sauce tastes (odd   oddly).
8. The Glockenspiel Quartet sounds (good   well) tonight.
9. The dog tasted the leftovers (cautious   cautiously).
10. Blindfolded, I felt my way (slow   slowly) through the coal mine.
11. When Rambette grows up, she hopes to become (notorious   notoriously).
12. The actors felt (weird   weirdly) in their cellophane costumes.

Test on Just About Everything So Far

Part I

Please identify the part of speech of each of the words in bold print in the Part II letter to Grandma Pringle:

Mongo _____

vacation _____

for _____

but _____

expensive _____

we _____

saw _____

we _____

too _____

never _____

Part II

Please find and correct *at least* 25 errors in the following letter (there are 50 or so— go wild!):

Dear Grandma Pringle,

    Myself and **Mongo** wanted you and Grandpa to know that wer'e having a good time here in the Hainesville Woods. Our **vacation** got off to a bad start, when the plane from Decatur was delayed **for** three days **but** we finally got here. In my opinion, I think that forests are more fun than costly **expensive** hotels. We seen 8 mooses yesterday **we** could of **saw** deers to but we was **too** tired from the trip. The guide told Mongo and I that he receiveded a medal from Pasture and Creek magazine last year but just between you and I he ca'nt guide hisself out of a paper sack, we had to help him read his compass. I haven't **never** seen such a incompetent guide but hes a freindly guy and his breakfast's smell wonderfully. He made a omelet out of birch bark for breakfast and it tasted good. It don't hardly bother us that he watched television in his tent, when he should of been helping us identify wierd birds. It takes one to identify one you have always said and your right Grandma. Well thats all for now we have to arise and get up at 5 A.M. tomorrow morning to go on a antler hunt.

Love from Mongo and myself,

Fedonia

Part III

Please use each of the following constructions in a separate sentence:

1. was taught _____

2. sounds good _____

3. sits _____

4. it lay _____

5. the plural of monkey _____

6. its _____

7. there are _____

8. there is _____

9. you are praised _____

10. if I were _____

11. it's _____

12. she's _____

13. too _____

14. the plural possessive of child _____

15. hardly _____

16. you and me _____

17. ; _____

18. ; therefore, _____

19. , so _____

20. the singular of thieves _____

21. have raised _____

22. has lain _____

23. the plural of country _____

24. whom _____

25. could have _____

26. torn _____

27. swam _____

28. they're _____

29. their _____

30. is heard _____

Part IV

Write separate sentences for each of the following verb forms:

1. *to go* in the third person singular, simple past tense

2. *to see* in the third person singular, present perfect tense

3. *to burst* in the third person singular, simple past, passive voice

4. *to sing* in the first person plural, future tense

5. *to eat* in the first person singular, present progressive tense

6. *to buy* in the third person plural, past perfect tense

7. *to write* in the second person plural, present progressive tense

8. *to call* in the third person singular, present tense, passive voice

9. *to raise* in the first person singular, simple past tense

10. *to lay* in the third person singular, future tense

Part V

In the following sentences, supply at least five zingy verbs to replace the verbs that are in italics:

1. They *said*, "Help!"
2. Carnivorous bushes *are* in my front yard.
3. The Martians *went* to the White House.

Part VI

Change the passive verbs to active verbs; make all other necessary changes.

1. The opera singer *was listened to* by thirty thousand fans.
2. I *was being hypnotized* by the ticking of the grandfather clock.

3. The bumblebee *was trapped* in a mayonnaise jar by the little girl.
4. The last clove cupcake *will be eaten* by Monstro, the walking disposal.
5. The contest *was won* by the Electric Kazoo Band.
6. Mrs. Pringle, the Mother of the Year, *is being hugged* by her ten children.
7. Our house *was built* in two hours by Mr. Coyote, the speedy carpenter.
8. The mayor *was informed* by his assistant that the crowd was hostile.
9. Mongo *will be drenched* by a water balloon at noon tomorrow.
10. The whistling janitor *was transferred* to the night shift by the personnel director.

Part VII

Look closely at these sentences, and fix anything you think needs fixing:

1. I haven't ever seen an unicorn.
2. Elmo thought the test was to hard.
3. The baby has finally went to sleep, and I can't hardly keep my eyes open.
4. You have broke my heart, but I have forgave you.
5. There's ten wildcats setting in our apple tree.
6. Rambette didn't talk to nobody, she had no fun at all.
7. I won't hardly know what to do, if your not here by twelve noon.
8. Their cat caught its tail in a swinging door, so they're going to take it to its doctor.
9. When he disagreed with me, I says, "Lose the attitude, Buster!"
10. If you don't go to the store tomorrow, we won't have nothing for lunch.

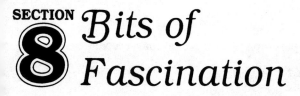

SECTION 8 *Bits of Fascination*

This section will concentrate on some intriguing aspects of English. You will learn about what happens to participles when they aren't accompanied by auxiliaries, you will laugh about dangling participles and misplaced modifiers, you will be introduced to the comparison of adjectives and adverbs, you will grow to appreciate parallelism, and you will learn about using certain words correctly.

There is a humdinger of a test at the end of this section.

PARTICIPLES WITHOUT AUXILIARIES

You have learned that both past and present participles must have auxiliaries in order to function as verbs.

Without an auxiliary, the past participle of a verb becomes an adjective:

Pursued by the vicious canary, the cat hid under the porch.
Hidden under the porch, the unlucky cat got stuck in some old gum.
Stuck in some old gum, the cat wailed piteously.

Without an auxiliary, the present participle (the *ing* one) may become either an adjective or a noun:

The **pursuing** canary looked insane with rage. **(adjective)**
The **hiding** cat whimpered and trembled. **(adjective)**
The gum **sticking** his paws together was like rubber cement. **(adjective)**

Pursuing cats is the canary's favorite sport. **(noun)**
Hiding under the porch was a smart thing for the cat to do. **(noun)**
Sticking his paws together with old gum was not the cat's idea of a good time. **(noun)**

Exercise

Please look closely at the following sentences to see if the participle is an adjective, a noun, or part of a verb. Write your answer beside the number.

Examples:

noun   *Digging* for buried treasure is a pirate's most strenuous job.

Adjective The *digging* pirate threw his back out of alignment.

Verb   He *had been digging* nonstop for a week.

_____ 1. *Running* through the meadow can be hazardous to your shoes.

_____ 2. The wildflowers tripped the *running* girl.

_____ 3. She *has been running* in meadows for six months.

_____ 4. Ms. Siberia *has been smiling* all year.

_____ 5. The *smiling* Ms. Siberia won the International Dental Derby.

_____ 6. *Smiling* is Ms. Siberia's only talent.

_____ 7. *Grown* to adulthood, Grandma Pringle's children have left home.

_____ 8. Mongo *has grown* six inches in six weeks.

_____ 9. He *has been growing* at an alarming rate for a year.

_____ 10. *Growing* boys need lots of chocolate chip cookies and smiles.

GERUNDS

When the present participle (the *ing* one) is used as a noun, it is called a **gerund.** Use the possessive form of a noun or pronoun that comes immediately before a gerund.

The **car's** stalling reduced Rambette to tears.
Your cooking is improving.
Santa's chuckling drove the reindeer crazy.

Exercise

Look carefully for gerunds in the following sentences and make sure that a noun or a pronoun immediately before the gerund is in the possessive form:

1. You falling asleep in the middle of my speech hurt my feelings.
2. Him driving at 175 miles per hour through town makes me nervous.
3. Mongo teasing his sister got him into a lot of trouble yesterday.
4. The canary chasing cats is not a good thing to do.
5. Them tying the babysitter to a tree is the last straw.

Make sure that the present participle is really functioning as a *noun* before you automatically use the possessive form before it. (Because the present participle looks the same whether it's being used as a noun, as an adjective, or as part of a verb, this takes some practice!)

The **woman wearing** a tuxedo irritated me.

means that the *woman* irritated you; "wearing a tuxedo" functions as an adjective here and identifies the irritating woman.

The **woman's wearing** a tuxedo irritated me.

means that *the wearing of the tuxedo* irritated you; *wearing* is a gerund here, and it serves as the subject of the sentence. (If the woman had worn something else, she probably wouldn't have bothered you a bit.)

PARTICIPIAL PHRASES

A group of words containing a participle is called a **participial phrase** (remember that a phrase doesn't have both a subject and a verb).

tiptoeing through the tulips
gone with the wind
flying for the first time

A participial phrase that comes first in a sentence must describe the subject of the sentence.

Tiptoeing through the tulips, I tripped over a big rock.
Gone with the wind, the banker's **hat** disappeared into the lake.
Flying for the first time, the nervous **passenger** prayed a lot.

When the participial phrase doesn't sensibly describe the subject of the sentence, the construction is called a **dangling participle.**

Tiptoeing through the tulips, the big **rock** tripped me.
(This has to mean that the *rock* was tiptoeing through the tulips, which is something straight out of the Twilight Zone!)

Gone with the wind, the **banker** lost his hat in the lake.
(This has to mean that the *banker* was picked up by the wind, which is straight out of Oz!)
Flying for the first time, a lot of **prayers** were said by the nervous passenger.
(This has to mean that the *prayers* were flying for the first time, which makes your hair hurt to think about.)

Beware of dangling participles; they can turn the most serious sentence into nonsense.

Remember Comma Rule 6: use a comma after a participial phrase beginning a sentence.

Exercise in Recognizing Dangling Participles

Look carefully at the following sentences. If the participial phrase describes the subject of the sentence sensibly, write *OK* beside the number and circle the subject that the participial phrase describes.

If the participle dangles (doesn't make sense when applied to the subject of the sentence), write *dang* beside the number and circle the subject of the sentence.

Examples:

_____*Dang*_____   Falling down the stairs, my (earlobe) was broken.
_____*OK*_____   Falling down the stairs, (I) broke my earlobe.

_____ 1. Written in the sand, high tide erased the message.

_____ 2. Written in the sand, the message disappeared at high tide.

_____ 3. Thrown into a kitchen drawer, I bent my slotted spoon.

_____ 4. Thrown into a kitchen drawer, my slotted spoon was bent.

_____ 5. Walking to church, my grandmother's cane broke.

_____ 6. Walking to church, my grandmother broke her cane.

_____ 7. Set to explode at noon, the bomb ticked in the belfry.

_____ 8. Set to explode at noon, my boss found a bomb in the belfry.

_____ 9. Sitting on a lilypad, we saw a frog yesterday.

_____ 10. Sitting on a lilypad, the frog was seen yesterday.

_____ 11. Lurking under the bed, the child was afraid of monsters.

_____ 12. Lurking under the bed, the monsters waited for the child to go to sleep.

_____ 13. Hung out to dry, the sheets looked like ghosts.

_____ 14. Hung out to dry, I saw ghosts on the clothesline.

_____ 15. Having blown a gasket, my car was towed to the service station.

_____ 16. Having blown a gasket, the mechanic fixed my car.

_____ 17. Swimming to shore, the boat rescued the sailor.

_____ 18. Swimming to shore, the sailor was rescued by the boat.

_____ 19. Running to catch the bus, my shoelace broke.

_____ 20. Running to catch the bus, I broke my shoelace.

SOME WORDS OF CAUTION

Sometimes, it's easier to turn a participial phrase into a dependent clause than to try to tinker with the rest of the sentence:

Falling into the puddle, my nose started to bleed.

We're in big trouble here; the participle dangles all over the place, and we're left with the notion that the nose did the falling all by itself. We have a couple of choices: we can say

Falling into the puddle, I started to get a nosebleed.

or

When I fell into the puddle, my nose started to bleed.

Don't feel that you have to preserve the participial phrase at all costs; you're always free to change it into a dependent clause.

Needless to say, a participial phrase can't hang out in the breeze all by itself and pretend to be a sentence.

We found the canary. Swallowing the cat's ear. (No!)

Simply hitch the participial phrase to the sentence right before it or to the sentence right after it, depending on which makes sense.

We found the canary swallowing the cat's ear. (Yes!)
Swallowing the cat's ear, we found the canary. (Yuck! You must have been very hungry!)
Exhausted and aching. Mr. Muscles fainted in aerobics class. (No!)
Exhausted and aching, Mr. Muscles fainted in aerobics class. (Yes!)

Please remember that a participle must be accompanied by an auxiliary verb to do the work of a verb.

I **have run** 50 miles today.
I **have been running** for 30 years.

MISPLACED MODIFIERS

Be sure to place descriptive words and phrases as close as you can to the words they describe; otherwise, your readers will be confused about what you really mean. Look at this bundle of bewilderment:

The boys gave a present to their mother wrapped in paper towels.

Does this mean that the *present* was wrapped in paper towels or that the boys' *mother* was wrapped in paper towels?

This can be clarified by moving the descriptive phrase right next to the word it describes:

The boys gave a present wrapped in paper towels to their mother.

Here's another package of puzzlement:

Grandma gave ice cream to the children covered with fudge sauce.

Do you suppose that the *ice cream* was covered with fudge sauce or that the *children* were covered with fudge sauce? When children are involved, anything is possible, but the sentence probably means that the *ice cream* was covered with fudge sauce.

We can fix this sentence by putting the descriptive phrase right next to the word it describes:

Grandma gave ice cream covered with fudge sauce to the children.

Here's one more case of confusion:

The man tripped over the canary with steel-toed boots on.

Who—the man or the canary—was wearing the steel-toed boots? Although we have been exposed to some wild and crazy canaries so far, the sentence probably means:

The man with steel-toed boots on tripped over the canary.

Exercise

If the descriptive phrase is already in the appropriate place, write *OK* beside the number. If the descriptive phrase is in the wrong place, circle the word that it describes and rewrite the sentence.

1. The ambulance drivers took the accident victim to the hospital *with the broken leg.*
2. The clown kissed the woman *with the red rubber nose.*
3. Steak was served by the chef *that was swimming in gravy.*
4. Rambo wore a headband *that had purple sequins on it.*
5. The nurse's uniform hung in the closet *that was stiff with starch.*

TWO-WAY ADVERBS

People who interrupt *constantly* annoy me.

Hmmmmmm. Which word—*interrupt* or *annoy*—does the adverb *constantly* modify? Does the sentence mean that people who *constantly interrupt* annoy me, or does it mean that people who interrupt *annoy* me *constantly*? Located where it is in the sentence, *constantly* can jump either way and attach itself either to *interrupt* or to *annoy*.

In your writing, try to be precise; make sure to place adverbs right next to the words you want them to accompany. Otherwise, your readers will become hopelessly confused and discouraged.

Exercise

Look carefully at the italicized adverbs in these sentences. If an adverb is in a two-way position, move it so that it modifies only one word.

1. People who love music *truly* dance well.
2. Anyone who watches television *frequently* sees commercials.
3. Adults who whine *often* are lonely.
4. People who exercise *seldom* have back trouble.
5. Students who forget their books *daily* are in trouble.

ONLY

Another small modifier that can cause a lot of confusion is *only*; its position in a sentence is crucial. Look at this bit of fascination:

Only I fed the parakeet yesterday.
(This means that nobody else fed him.)
I **only** fed the parakeet yesterday.
(This means that I didn't sing to him or bathe him—I just fed him.)
I fed **only** the parakeet yesterday.
(This means I didn't feed the python or the giraffe or anything but the parakeet.)
I fed the **only** parakeet yesterday.
(This means that the poor bird has no brothers or sisters; he's an only parakeet.)
I fed the parakeet **only** yesterday.
(This means that the parakeet was fed recently, and I'm astonished that he's clutching his throat in terminal hunger-pangs already.)
I fed the parakeet yesterday **only**.
(This means that it's someone else's responsibility to feed him the rest of the time.)

Because **only** is such a small word, it's easy to fling it around carelessly, but you should be cautious with its placement, now that you know it's so important. You might catch yourself saying something like "I only paid $200 for my car" when you really mean "I paid only $200 for my car."

PARALLELISM

Parallelism (or **parallel structure**) means that words, phrases, or clauses in a pair or in a series are of the same grammatical kind:

           adjective adjective   adjective
Scouts are brave, clean, and reverent.

            noun   noun   noun
Mongo likes snakes, snails, and worms.

              infinitive   infinitive
Cinderella was told to sweep the dungeon and to clean the moat.

Parallelism is one of the characteristics of a good, clear, considerate, courteous, precise writer. A writer who is striving for perfection must have a thorough grasp of phrases, clauses, verb forms, and parts of speech.

      Lack of parallelism can be very irritating and confusing to readers; when they take the time and trouble to read something, they expect to find symmetry and balance. Readers lose patience when they have to cope with something like this:

              infinitive infinitive   gerund
My grandmother likes to camp, to fish, and skydiving.   .

A writer who cares about parallelism could fix this in either of two ways:

              infinitive infinitive   infinitive
My grandmother likes to camp, to fish, and to skydive:

or

              gerund   gerund   gerund
My grandmother likes camping, fishing, and skydiving.

Exercise

In the sentences below, choose your favorite way to achieve parallel structure, making sure that words, phrases, or clauses in a pair or in a series match grammatically.

Example:

Lizzo is healthy, wealthy, and a wise person. (not parallel)

Lizzo is healthy, wealthy, and wise. (parallel)

or

Lizzo is a healthy, wealthy, wise person. (parallel)

  1. Ma praised Mongo for being thoughtful and promptness.

2.   Skeeter McClure is small, quick, and an athlete.

---

3.   He promised to clean his room and that he would take out the trash.

---

4.   Riding the bus is less expensive than to drive a car.

---

5.   The old house needs new wiring, new insulation, and to be given a new coat of paint.

DEGREES OF ADJECTIVES AND ADVERBS

Adjectives and adverbs have three degrees of comparison: the **positive, comparative,** and **superlative.**

The **positive degree** is just the plain old adjective or adverb.

Rambette is **happy.**
Turtle O'Hara moves **slowly.**

The **comparative degree** is used for comparisons between two items.

Rambette is **happier** than a speckled pup.
Turtle O'Hara moves **more slowly** than Wyle E. Coyote.

The **superlative degree** is used for comparisons among more than two items.

Rambette is the **happiest** woman in the Ozark Mountains.
Turtle O'Hara moves the **most slowly** of all the members of the Take Time to Smell the Flowers Club.

Adjectives and adverbs of one syllable form their comparative and superlative degrees by adding *er* and *est.*

Positive	Comparative	Superlative
strong	strong**er**	strong**est**
fast	fast**er**	fast**est**

Some adjectives of two syllables form their comparative and superlative degrees by adding *er* and *est;* other adjectives of two syllables form their comparative and superlative degrees by inserting *more* and *most* in front. (A large dictionary will help you with these forms.)

Positive	Comparative	Superlative
pretty	prettier	prettiest
handsome	more handsome	most handsome

Adjectives of more than two syllables and adverbs ending in *ly* form their comparative and superlative degrees with *more* and *most*.

Positive	Comparative	Superlative
beautiful	more beautiful	most beautiful
difficult	more difficult	most difficult
easily	more easily	most easily

MORE ABOUT DEGREES OF ADJECTIVES AND ADVERBS

Use *less* and *least* to indicate less or least of a quality:

Positive	Comparative	Superlative
rocky	less rocky	least rocky
slyly	less slyly	least slyly

There are a few adjectives and adverbs that don't follow the regular rules for the comparative and superlative degrees. It won't take long to memorize these irregular forms:

Positive	Comparative	Superlative
bad	worse	worst
good	better	best
well	better	best
many	more	most
much	more	most

Beware of double comparisons, ones in which the degree is formed twice by adding *er* or *est* using *more* or *most*. Here are some horrible examples:

He is **more** young**er** than your grandfather.
That was the **most** unkind**est** insult of all.

More and *most* are unnecessary in these sentences; the *er* and *est* take care of the degree of comparison.

Beware of incomplete comparisons. When you use the comparative or superlative degree of an adjective or adverb, make sure that your readers know what's being compared. Here are some more horrible examples:

My boss likes recruiting better. (Better than what?—hiring? firing? tapdancing? root-canal work?)
Illinois is nicer. (Nicer than what?—Antarctica? a compost heap? the Garden of Eden? Death Valley?)

Please remember to use the **comparative form** for comparisons between *two* items:

Dweezle, my old**er** child, saves thyme in a bottle.
(The writer has *two* children.)

Remember to use the **superlative form** for comparisons among *more than two* items:

Dweezle, my old**est** child, saves thyme in a bottle.
(The writer has *more than two* children.)

Exercise in Degrees of Adjectives and Adverbs

Please supply the comparative and superlative forms:

Positive	Comparative	Superlative
cheerful		
much		
wonderful		
cautiously		
nice		
eager		
good		
splendid		
many		
quietly		
shyly		
generous		
well		
apathetic		
flexible		
fascinating		
hypnotically		
enormous		
ambitious		
lackadaisically		
rude		
unsuccessful		
courageous		
bad		
late		

USING WORDS CORRECTLY

The next few pages explore some of the errors that people frequently make in speaking and writing. Some will be new to you, and some won't, but familiarity with all of them will help you become a precise speaker and writer.

A lot

A lot—two words. Some people are fond of writing things like "I've had alot of trouble with my car." Perhaps they're confused because there is a verb, *to allot*, which means *to apportion*. If this is one of your writing habits, leave an extra space between the *a* and the *lot* until you're comfortable with *a lot*.

Etc.

Etc. is an abbreviation of two Latin words: *et cetera*. In Latin, *et* means *and; cetera* means *other things*. Therefore, *et cetera* literally means *and other things*, which is precisely what we want when we use it at the ends of long lists.

And etc. makes no sense at all; it says *and and other things*, for the *et* part of *etc.* already means *and*.

People who don't know the Latin origin of *etc.* sometimes write *ect*, which is wrong.

Ain't

Yes, *ain't* is in the dictionary, but that doesn't mean that it is an acceptable word. The dictionary merely includes words that people use, and, unfortunately, some people use *ain't*. Please don't say or write *ain't*. If you're truly emotionally attached to the word, go into your closet in the morning and say it as many times as you need to in order to get through the day, but don't let it cross your lips outside of your closet.

The reason is that

Some people say and write *the reason is because*, but that has a built-in repetition. The word *reason* already implies *because*, so there is no need for *because* after *reason*. The correct term is *the reason is that*.

If you use the word *reason*, don't use *because*:

My **reason** for not becoming a rock star is **that** I'm allergic to sequins.

If you use *because*, don't use *reason*:

I won't become a rock star **because** I'm allergic to sequins.

Wait for

Some Midwesterners and Southerners are fond of saying *wait on* when they really mean *wait for*. To *wait on* means *to serve*, as in

Alice waited on 350 customers at the Tofu Tepee last night.

To *wait for* means just what it says: to delay action until something or someone else is ready, as in

I'll wait for you at the airport.

Used to and Supposed to

When they are followed by *to*, the words *use* and *suppose* must have a *d* at the end (even though you never really hear it when it's said):

He use**d** to be a couch potato, but he's now an obsessive jogger.
You were suppose**d** to buy milk and eggs on your way home.

Where (~~at~~)

Try not to tack *at* onto a statement or a question that includes the word *where*. *Where* already has the idea of *at* built in, so saying or writing *where at* is a hideous example of word pollution.

If you are in the habit of saying *where at*, bite your tongue before *at* can pass your lips.

Where did you get your pink satellite dish ~~at~~?
The classroom is where the action is ~~at~~.

Like and As

Use *like* when it is not followed by a clause:

I wish I could skydive **like** my sister Kate.

Use *as* when it is followed by a clause:

I wish I could skydive **as** my sister Kate does.

Like in these situations is a preposition, so a pronoun that follows it must be in the objective case:

Beverly and Renata sing just like **me.**

Because a clause must follow *as*, the pronoun must be in the nominative (subject) case:

Beverly and Renata sing just as **I** do.

Fewer and Less and Amount and Number

Use *number* and *fewer* when you're referring to things that can be counted individually.

The **number** of terrorist canaries has increased recently.
There are **fewer** terrorist canaries in Arkansas than in Illinois.

Use *amount* and *less* when you're referring to things that *can't* be counted individually:

Being a canary inspector can cause a great **amount** of stress.
There is **less** stress involved in being a snake milker than in being a canary inspector.

Here's a handy hint: Use *fewer* and *number* when you're dealing with words in the **plural form**—fewer students, number of students; fewer parking spaces, number of parking spaces. Use *less* and *amount* when you're dealing with words in the **singular form**—less grief, amount of grief; less joy, amount of joy.

Different from and Different than

You will dazzle all those with whom you communicate if you develop the habit of using *different from* instead of *different than* except when a clause follows:

Your concrete canoe is **different from** mine.
My wombat is **different from** all the rest.
The campsite looks **different than** it did last year.
This butterscotch pizza tastes **different than** it did yesterday.

Regardless

Perhaps you have heard and seen the word *irregardless*, which is a one-word double negative. *Ir* is a negative prefix, and *less* is a negative suffix, so poor old *regard* is attacked from both ends by negatives, and the word that results has no meaning whatsoever (at least on this planet); perhaps people confuse it with *irrespective*, which is a perfectly legitimate word because it doesn't have a negative at each end.
The word that you want to mean *without regard* is *regardless*.

Regardless of my warnings, Mongo stepped on the crack; his mother has been in traction ever since.

Bust

Bust is always a noun; it can refer to a part of the female anatomy or to a statue that consists only of a head and shoulders.
Bust is never an acceptable verb; it exists in slang as a synonym for *to arrest,*

but many people mistakenly think that *to bust* is a synonym for *to break*. It isn't. It isn't a synonym for *to burst*, either.

The bubble **burst** when the dog snapped at it.
The pitcher **broke** his New Year's resolution to give up bubblegum.

To aggravate

Technically, *to aggravate* means *to make heavier* or *to make worse*; it doesn't mean *to irritate* or *to annoy*.

The parrot's squawking aggravated my headache.
(This means that the squawking made my *headache* worse, which makes sense.)

Watch out for this, though:

The parrot's squawking aggravated me.
(Whoa! This means that the squawking made *me* worse or heavier, which can make your head sting to think about!)

Either of these would be fine:

The parrot's squawking **irritated** me.
The parrot's squawking **annoyed** me.

Everyday and *Every day*

Everyday is an adjective that means *ordinary* or *routine:*

Come check out The Bargain Barn's **everyday** low prices!

Every day is an adverb that tells when:

The Bargain Barn has low prices **every day.**

(Now that you're aware of this, you'll be amazed at how often you'll notice newspaper ads using *everyday* as an adverb.)

Between and *Among*

You have already seen this distinction in action on pages 148 and 149, but it's important enough to repeat.
Use *between* with two items:

You'll have to choose **between** the BMW and the Mercedes.

Use *among* with more than two items:

You'll have to choose **among** the BMW, the Mercedes, the Ferrari, and the Ford.

Then and *Than*

Then refers to time:

Please muzzle the canary first; **then** milk the rattlesnake.

Than appears in comparisons:

I've got belt buckles that are older **than** you, sonny.

Anxious and *Eager*

Many people seem to think that *anxious* and *eager* have the same meaning, but there's a big difference. The primary meanings of *anxious* involve worry and uneasiness, so

I'm anxious to see you.

means that the thought of seeing you causes feelings of worry and uneasiness in me—there is not just unbounded joy here.
 On the other hand, *eager* suggests strong desire or interest, so

I'm eager to see you.

doesn't have any negative overtones; it means that I really want to see you.

Too adjective *of a* noun

You have probably heard people say things like:

That's too big **of** a job for one person.

or

He's too good **of** a runner to lose the race.

or

That's too steep **of** a hill for Grandma Pringle to climb.

or

It's not that big **of** a deal to me.

 The *of* in the above sentences is unnecessary—it just takes time and energy to write or say, and it doesn't contribute to the meaning of the sentence. Omit the *of*, and you'll have:

That's too big a job for one person.

and

He's too good a runner to lose the race.

and

That's too steep a hill for Grandma Pringle to climb.

and

It's not that big a deal to me.

(For such a small word, *of* certainly gets into a lot of trouble—remember when it was trying to be an auxiliary verb: "I should *of* called first"?)

Farther and *Further*

Use *farther* when you're talking about actual *distance:*

We were all half dead by sunset, but the bus driver wanted to go fifty miles **farther.**
I live **farther** from the Shop-o-Rama than you do.

Use *further* when you're talking about *extent:*

I'd like to explore your excuse a bit **further.**
We plan to do **further** research into the vampire reports.

Nauseated and *Nauseous*

Have you ever heard someone say "Anchovies make me nauseous" or "I can't go to class because I feel nauseous"? The person really meant to say "Anchovies are nauseous" or "I can't go to class because I feel nauseated." *Nauseous* actually means *sickening; nauseated* means *feeling queasy.* Therefore, a person who complains of feeling nauseous is actually admitting to feeling sickening (capable of making someone else feel sick). All kinds of horrible things can be nauseous even to think about—oysters in whipped cream, anchovies with chocolate sauce, a rollercoaster ride—but they make a person feel nauseated; people are very seldom nauseous.

Exercise in Using Words Correctly

From the choice in parentheses, please circle the correct word or words in the following sentences:

1. Before you leave for work, please make the beds, wash the dishes, turn off the stove, close the refrigerator door, (etc.   and etc.)
2. You have too big (a   of a) lawn for me to mow in an hour.
3. The wombat's whimpering (aggravated   irritated) my bad mood.

4. The wombat's whimpering (aggravated   irritated) me.

5. Divide the sweepstakes prize (between   among) your two children.

6. Divide the sweepstakes prize (between   among) your four children.

7. I plan to wear my (everyday   every day) clothes to the mudwrestling match.

8. I mudwrestle (everyday   every day).

9. Mongo fell out of a tree and (broke   busted) his watch.

10. I'm flying to Tucson next week; I'll call you (than   then).

11. Fedonia ate ten corn dogs, four banana splits, and a package of marshmallows; no wonder she feels (nauseous   nauseated).

12. Mongo would rather set his hair on fire and eat steel wool (than   then) listen to Rambo.

13. Where did you buy your purple (parachute at   parachute)?

14. (Irregardless   Regardless) of his allergies, Sneezy fills the house with bouquets of goldenrod and ragweed.

15. "Cannibals Shrink Space Alien's Head" is a headline that demands (farther   further) investigation.

16. This express checkout-line is for ten items or (less   fewer).

17. If you get to the theater before I do, please wait (on   for) me.

18. Weren't you (suppose   supposed) to pay the phone bill last week?

19. The reason I went to sleep was (because   that) the classroom was too warm.

20. Your house is different (from   than) theirs.

21. Just (as   like) I predicted, she's being promoted.

22. Your sister is tall and slim; don't you wish you looked like (she   her)?

23. As a lineman for the county, you should climb (fewer   less) poles.

24. The chef has (a lot   alot) of thyme on his hands.

25. Mongo (use   used) to be afraid of spiders; they're his best friends now.

26. I can't walk one step (further   farther) without a new shoelace.

Test—Absolutely the Last One on Just About Everything Essential

Part I

Please create a complex sentence that contains at least one common noun, one proper noun, one pronoun, two verbs, one adjective, one definite article, one indefinite article, one adverb, and one preposition. Underline and label the requested parts of speech; then write the rule number above any comma or semicolon in your sentence.

_____

_____

_____

Part II

Examine the following sentences to see if there is a dangling participle or a misplaced modifier; rewrite any sentence that has these faults. If a sentence is correct, please write *OK* beside the number.

1. Watching the movie, the seat collapsed.
2. The man picked the rose wearing a denim jacket.
3. Falling into the canyon, my ear started to ache.
4. Eating popcorn, the bowl slipped out of my hand.
5. The bee stung the girl with the beehive hairdo.
6. The girl climbed the tree with the ponytail.
7. Salad was served by the hostess covered with Italian dressing.
8. Driving my pickup, a toad got run over.
9. Smelling the flowers in the meadow, the bull chased me.
10. Smelling the flowers in the meadow, I was chased by the bull.
11. The women kissed the sailors with orange skirts on.
12. Swinging through the trees, Tarzan's famous yell was heard.
13. Singing in the shower, I dropped the soap.
14. Cleaning the house, she found dust bunnies everywhere.
15. The man got stuck in a phone booth dressed as Superman.

Part III

Look closely at these sentences; fix anything you think needs fixing.

1. Fedonia is weird, she likes to cook, to vacuum, and ironing dishtowels.
2. I couldn't hardly hear the siren, because the wind was making to much noise.

3. Mongos favorite movie is Night of the Living Tree Toads, and plus Mongos' favorite television show is Leave It to Weasel.

4. The Savings Silo has very, low every day prices for new truck buyers.

5. Mister Blister the camp director said, "I should of sended you home you little mischief maker because you let wild geeses eat the side of you're tent.

Part IV

Please use each of the following constructions in a separate sentence:

1. between you and her

_____

2. aggravated

_____

3. that hard a question

_____

4. everyday

_____

5. he lay

_____

6. hardly

_____

7. waitresses'

_____

8. church's

_____

9. whose

_____

10. who's

_____

11. taking

_____

12. ; therefore,

_____

13.   , but

_____

14.   too (meaning also)

_____

15.   too (meaning excessively)

_____

16.   its

_____

17.   it's

_____

18.   to think, to plan, and to dream

_____

19.   might have burst

_____

20.   used to

_____

21.   supposed to

_____

22.   like your sister

_____

23.   further

_____

24.   different from

_____

25.   different than

_____

26.   had been sitting

_____

27.   will be raising

_____

28.   their

_____

SECTION 9 *Paragraphs*

Now that you have learned the fundamentals of English and the requirements of a good, clear sentence, you can enjoy putting sentences together in a longer unit of composition, the paragraph. Although paragraphs are usually parts of an essay, which is a still longer unit of composition, practice in writing single, self-contained paragraphs can help you get ready to write essays. This section will discuss the essential elements of a paragraph and will give you practice both in recognizing a good paragraph when you see one and in writing some of your own.

A FEW WORDS ABOUT FIGURATIVE LANGUAGE

Before we get into this section, which will give you a lot of practice in writing paragraphs, it's helpful to be familiar with figurative language (sometimes known as figures of speech) in order to increase your options for clarity and vividness in your writing. While literal statements are straightforward and factual, figurative statements are dramatic and forceful, seeking to present reality in a new way. For example, here's a literal statement:

As I try to write, I can think of nothing to say.

Here's a figurative statement.

As I try to write, my mind is a blank slab of black asphalt.

My mind is a blank slab of black asphalt is called a **metaphor** (pronounced MET-ah-four), a figure of speech that *equates essentially unlike things:*

The teacher is a caged tiger, pacing back and forth at the front of the classroom.
My life is a three-ring circus.

To be successful, figurative language must be fresh and natural, enhancing the writer's meaning. Metaphors have to be handled with extreme caution in order to avoid a **mixed metaphor,** in which the writer seems to lose track of the qualities and characteristics of the first metaphor.

She often hatched new projects, using them as springboards for the ladder of success.

(We start out with the image of baby birds, then they turn into something that adds power to a jump, and we end up with a ladder that has been launched by a springboard. Doesn't this make your hair hurt?)

A **simile** (pronounced SIM-ill-lee) is a figure of speech that usually begins with the words *like* or *as,* and it *compares essentially different things:*

My hair looks **like a barbed-wire fence in a hurricane.**
She's as busy **as a double-jointed woodpecker in a lumber yard.**
I feel **like a vulture's lunch.**

A **cliché** (pronounced klee-SHAY) is an expression (often a simile) that has been *repeated so often* that it no longer provides a fresh, new way of saying something. Do the following expressions sound hauntingly familiar?

cool as a cucumber
fresh as a daisy
gentle as a lamb
wise as an owl
crazy as a loon
busy as a bee
neat as a pin
pretty as a picture
strong as an ox
sick as a dog
dry as a bone
old as the hills
clear as a bell

Because clichés are so familiar to all of us, using them in your writing lulls your readers into thinking that they already know what you're going to say; you're using prefabricated expressions instead of your own fresh, new perspectives. Try to avoid clichés in speaking and in writing.

Hyperbole (pronounced high-PER-bo-lee), *extravagant exaggeration*, is another useful figure of speech to know about:

If I've told you once, I've told you a million times to close the screen door.
I'm going **to fold, mutilate, and spindle him** if he bothers me again.
I'm so hungry **I could eat a horse.**
This suitcase weighs **a ton.**

Personification is a figure of speech in which *objects and ideas behave in human ways:*

My house gobbles up my paycheck faster than I can earn it.
I could hear the **murmuring** of **waves** at the beach, **impatiently waiting** their turn **to kiss** the shore.
Love stuck its foot into the aisle of my life and tripped me.

Don't think that good writing has to include figurative language tossed in like salt and pepper; however, when a way of putting words together occurs to you that will help your readers see, hear, feel, or think exactly as you want them to, don't hesitate to use it.

THE ESSENTIAL ELEMENTS OF A PARAGRAPH

A **paragraph** is made up of related sentences in logical order that develop one main idea. The **topic sentence** of the paragraph states the main idea, and it is usually a general statement; the body of the paragraph develops and clarifies the topic sentence by giving supporting details and specific examples. A good paragraph has a **concluding sentence** that brings the development of the topic sentence to a satisfying close. Each sentence in the paragraph must be related to the topic sentence.

PARAGRAPH FORM AND LENGTH

Indent the first line of a paragraph five spaces on a typewriter or about half an inch in handwriting; write the rest of the paragraph from margin to margin, with no more indentations. A paragraph doesn't need a title because the topic you are writing about should be obvious in your first sentence.

A paragraph has no one absolutely correct length; it must be long enough to develop the promise of the topic sentence adequately, but it should be short enough to be interesting. When you're writing a rough draft of a paragraph, it's a good idea to aim for from eight to ten sentences, but your polished paragraph might have only seven sentences, or it might have fifteen. The length really depends on the topic you have chosen to develop.

The whole purpose of writing is to convey your thoughts about a topic; if possible, you should choose to write about something that interests you, so you can share something of yourself with your readers.

THE TOPIC SENTENCE

The foundation of a paragraph is the **topic sentence;** it tells your readers what you plan to discuss, and it gets them interested and curious. The topic sentence is usually a general statement that is made specific by the sentences in the body of the paragraph. Your topic sentence makes a promise to your readers, and the rest of the paragraph works to fulfill that promise.

Because the job of a paragraph is to develop one main thought, your topic sentence shouldn't promise more than your paragraph can deliver. For instance,

Human beings have been involved in many conflicts since the beginning of recorded time.

is doomed as a paragraph's topic sentence because it promises far more than a paragraph can deliver—the explanation of such an extensive topic would require several books.

Look at this as a possible topic sentence for a manageable paragraph:

I still feel bad about an argument I had at work last week.

The author can give supporting details about the bad feeling and specific examples of what the argument was about and who was involved.

Once you have created a good topic sentence, the rest of the paragraph practically writes itself. The topic sentence sets the boundaries of your paragraph for you—you can't go outside the limits placed on your paragraph by the topic sentence, but you must be sure to cover the important territory within those limits.

Although a topic sentence can appear anywhere in a paragraph, it's a good idea—while you're practicing—to make your topic sentence the first sentence. Go ahead and underline it, too, so you can easily keep referring to it to make sure that you're still on the right track.

Exercise in Recognizing Topic Sentences

Please read the following groups of scrambled statements and then underline the one sentence in each group that serves as a topic sentence for the rest of the ideas.

A.

1. I usually end up on the telephone instead.
2. My mind goes blank.
3. I forget how to spell the simplest words.
4. I can never find any stationery.
5. All the pens in the house either disappear or run dry just when I need one.
6. I can't think of anything interesting to say.
7. My letters usually end up sounding like old weather reports.
8. I don't like to write personal letters.
9. I don't know what sort of mood the person I'm writing to is in.

10. On the telephone, the person I'm talking with takes over at least half of the conversation.

B.

1. It makes me look like a toucan.
2. It turns bright red in the sun and in the cold.
3. It seems too large for the rest of my face.
4. My nose is the one thing I would change about myself if I could.
5. My family teases me about it all the time.
6. My brother says that it provides shade for miles around in the summertime.
7. My cousin calls me "the Beezer."
8. My mother tries to make me feel better by saying that my nose looks noble and Roman, but my sister says that it's Roman, all right—roamin' all over my face.
9. If I had a different nose, maybe I could be an anchor on the television news.
10. I could have died of embarrassment when my broadcasting instructor said that I have a nose for news, but she didn't mean to be cruel.
11. I think I'll start saving my money to have my nose made smaller.

RELATED SENTENCES

Look carefully at the following sentences:

1. I'm the only person I know of who has ever fallen asleep while riding a bicycle in the snow.
2. There are nine calories in each gram of fat.
3. Roses should be watered at their bases, not from above.
4. Augusta is the capital of Maine.
5. The original London Bridge was made of wood.
6. Contrary to popular belief, a snake's skin is velvety, not slimy.
7. My nephew was disappointed when he visited San Francisco because he didn't see any gravel pits.

Although each of these seven sentences is clear and potentially interesting, not one has even the slightest thing to do with any of the other six; they are totally unrelated. These seven sentences, therefore, can't make a paragraph because all the sentences in a paragraph must be related.

LOGICAL ORDER

The sentences in a paragraph should be in logical order, each sentence leading smoothly to the next until the promise of the topic sentence is fulfilled.

1. When the alarm clock screamed at 5 A.M., I couldn't believe it.

2. I dreaded winter, though, because there was always a lot of snow.
3. I stayed up till four o'clock one Sunday morning, studying for a big test that I was to take on Monday.
4. The job was actually very pleasant in the spring and in the fall.
5. It's very hard to ride a bike in the snow, especially when the bike's basket is full of newspapers.
6. Since I had 40 customers, I had to start my route at 5:30 A.M. on Sundays.
7. When I was in college, I earned a little extra money by delivering *The New York Times* to people in the community.
8. There was a blizzard raging outside; nevertheless, I loaded my bike basket with newspapers and started off.
9. On Sundays, my customers complained if they didn't have their papers by 7 A.M.
10. I'm the only person I know of who has ever fallen asleep while riding a bicycle in the snow.
11. I woke up just in time to see all of my newspapers being scattered over the mountains by the howling wind.
12. Now, 30 years later, whenever I settle down to read the Sunday *New York Times*, I still remember the day I fell asleep on my bike.
13. I remember starting to coast down one slippery hill and then waking up in a snowdrift at the bottom.

Although these 13 sentences are related, they are not in logical order. If sentence 10 were sentence 1, we would know immediately what the sentences have in common. Just for fun, make sentence 10 sentence 1, and then arrange the rest of the sentences in an order that seems logical to you.

SUPPORTING DETAILS

A good paragraph contains supporting details to develop the main thought that is expressed in the topic sentence. Look at this vat of vagueness:

Cows terrify me. You can't go anywhere in the country without

seeing a lot of cows. I don't mind snakes all that much, and spiders

are OK, but cows scare me to death. I don't even like milk.

Aren't you just wild to know why the author is so afraid of cows? The topic sentence promises to tell us, but, by the end of this very short paragraph, we don't know any more about why cows are so terrifying than we did before we started reading it. The author could have a great time telling of the personal experience with cows that led up to such a statement—specific examples would help to fulfill the promise of the topic sentence.

Just for practice, supply five sentences of supporting detail for the topic sentence about cows:

1. _____

2. _____

_____

3. _____

_____

4. _____

_____

5. _____

_____

IRRELEVANT INFORMATION

Each sentence in a paragraph should be related to the topic sentence. When you're writing a rough draft of a paragraph, it's comfortable to let the thoughts leave your head, travel down your arm, and end up on paper, and that's fine—that's what drafts are for. Actually, there's a stage of writing that comes before even the rough draft; it's called a "zero draft," and no one sees it but you. Zero drafts are useful for mental doodling, and they can kick-start your creative process by allowing you to jot down every thought that comes into your head about a topic. Because no one but you sees the zero draft, you can write it on anything—on a paper napkin with a ketchup-dipped French fry, with lipstick on a grocery sack, with your finger in the dust under your bed. After you've written the zero draft, it's wise to put it away for a day, so it can ripen. When you look at it again, you'll be able to decide what parts you want to keep and what parts should be shredded; once you start this decision process, you have progressed from the zero-draft stage to the rough-draft stage. When you're ready to polish and refine your paragraph for others to read, it's important to take a hard look at what you've written and to leave out sentences that don't help to fulfill the promise of your topic sentence. Look at this paragraph and cross out the sentences that, interesting though they may be, have nothing to do with the topic sentence and actually disrupt the flow.

2
Contrary to popular belief, a snake's skin is velvety, not slimy. When I was little, my favorite toy was a terrycloth snake that my mother made for
3
me. There was a snake that lived under our barn, too, and on hot summer
4
days, he would sunbathe on a rock in the pasture. I named him "Norman,"
5
but he wouldn't come when I called him. Once, when I was in fifth grade, someone put a snake in my desk at school, and when I reached in to get my
6
work, I touched him. His quick motion startled me, but after I calmed us both down, I stroked his skin and was surprised at how soft and smooth it
7
was. I guess I had expected it to be damp and slimy, but it reminded me of

8

the green velvet draperies in my grandmother's living room. If more people could actually touch snakes, perhaps they wouldn't automatically be repelled by them.

Please write four more sentences that will help make the paragraph more effective by adding supporting detail:

1. _____

_____

2. _____

_____

3. _____

_____

4. _____

_____

Additional Exercises for Recognizing Irrelevant Sentences in Paragraphs

A. Circle the number beside each sentence that should not be included in the polished version of a paragraph with the topic sentence "The world would be a better place if Mondays were eliminated."

1. The weekend would be a day longer.
2. There would be something on television in the evening besides football.
3. I was born on a Monday.
4. Tuesdays aren't all that terrific, either.
5. Employers complain that there is a lot of absenteeism on Mondays.
6. Cars that are made on Mondays are likely to be lemons.
7. Monday got its name from "Moon Day."
8. A lot of restaurants are closed on Mondays.
9. Many students cut Monday morning classes.
10. People often blame their mistakes on the fact that it's Monday.

B. Circle the number beside each sentence that should not be included in the polished version of a paragraph with the topic sentence "Cats are better pets than dogs."

1. Cats don't dig holes in the back yard for people to fall into.
2. Cats don't howl at the moon.
3. The ancient Egyptians revered cats.
4. Cats don't bark at the letter carrier.

5. Catwoman was a nifty character in the *Batman* show.
6. Cats don't smell bad when they're wet.
7. My mother says that my aunt makes catty remarks.
8. My favorite song is "Kitten on the Keys."
9. Cats discourage mice from living in the house.
10. Cats don't have to be taken for a walk twice a day.
11. Cats purr to let you know when they're happy; they don't wag their tails and knock all the knick-knacks off the furniture.

THE CONCLUDING SENTENCE OF A PARAGRAPH

The last sentence in your paragraph should let your reader know that you have fulfilled the promise of your topic sentence. The reader should feel satisfied and shouldn't have to turn your paper over to see if there's anything on the back, nor feel the need to hold your paper up to the light to see if you have written your conclusion in invisible ink. Above all, the reader should not be sent off on a new line of thought in the concluding sentence of a self-contained paragraph.

The following, tempting though they might be, are not good concluding sentences:

This is the end of my paragraph.
Well, that's about all I have to say.
I have to go now; my grandmother's calling me.
My pen is running out of ink.
That's all, folks!
Boy, am I ever glad this paragraph is over.
This is the concluding sentence of my paragraph.
I have worked on this paragraph for eighteen hours, so I'm quitting.
See you later!
Bye, now.

Which of the following do you think is the most satisfactory concluding sentence for a paragraph that begins with the topic sentence "There are nine calories in each gram of fat"? Circle the number of the sentence you choose.

1. This means goodbye forever, butter!
2. All in all, people who don't want to gain weight should be very careful with butter, margarine, and salad dressings.
3. No wonder Aunt Matilda is so huge—she eats lard for breakfast, lunch, and dinner.
4. I don't know what a gram is without "tele-" or "candy-" in front of it.
5. Fat, schmatt! You go around only once, so grab for the grease!

DIFFERENT KINDS OF PARAGRAPHS

Now that you are aware of the essential elements of a self-contained paragraph, you'll be interested to know that there are several kinds of paragraphs. We'll be working with four major categories:

Persuasive   A persuasive paragraph attempts to persuade your readers to agree with you; it contains solid reasons for your viewpoint.

Explanatory   An explanatory paragraph explains a procedure or an opinion. Again, your paragraph needs specific examples, so your readers can clearly understand what you're telling them.

Descriptive   A descriptive paragraph describes a person, place, animal, sensation, emotion, event, etc., so your readers can visualize or experience what you're describing. Descriptive paragraphs need precise and lively language; figurative language can be especially helpful.

Narrative   A narrative paragraph tells a story from your point of view.

Logical development, specific examples, and precise, lively language will make your paragraphs enjoyable to write and to read.

TOPICS FOR YOUR OWN PARAGRAPHS

Look at the following lists of topics and make a checkmark beside the *one* in each category that most interests you.

Persuasive Topics
1. an advantage of owning a pet
2. a disadvantage of owning a pet
3. an advantage of owning your home
4. a disadvantage of owning your home
5. an advantage of renting your home
6. a disadvantage of renting your home
7. an advantage of owning a car in the city
8. a disadvantage of owning a car in the city
9. an advantage of being part of a large family
10. a disadvantage of being part of a large family
11. one reason that people should have to retire at the age of 50
12. one reason that people should not have to retire at the age of 50
13. an advantage of a college education
14. a disadvantage of a college education
15. one reason that learning a foreign language is important

16. one reason that children under the age of ten should have their television-watching supervised

17. one reason that children under the age of ten should not have their television-watching supervised

18. one reason that elementary school should be in session all year, including the summer

19. one reason that elementary school should not be in session all year, including the summer

20. one reason that the voting age should be raised to 25

21. one reason that the voting age should not be raised to 25

22. one reason that tobacco advertising should be forbidden in the United States

23. one reason that tobacco advertising should not be forbidden in the United States

24. one reason that every business establishment that has 15 or more employees should have a child-care facility on the premises

25. one reason that every business establishment that has 15 or more employees should not have a child-care facility on the premises

26. one advantage of being female at the end of the twentieth century

27. one disadvantage of being female at the end of the twentieth century

28. one advantage of being male at the end of the twentieth century

29. one disadvantage of being male at the end of the twentieth century

30. one advantage of living in a small town

31. one disadvantage of living in a small town

32. one advantage of living in a city

33. one disadvantage of living in a city

34. the most needed change in America's welfare system

35. one reason that police officers should use tranquilizer pellets instead of bullets

36. one reason that police officers should not use tranquilizer pellets instead of bullets

37. one way the federal government could help farmers

38. one reason that school children should be bused to achieve racial integration

39. one reason that school children should not be bused to achieve racial integration

40. one reason that going to a theater to see a movie is more fun than watching a video of the movie at home

41. one reason that watching a video of a movie at home is more fun than going to a theater to see the movie

42. one reason that people over the age of 65 should have their driver's licenses cancelled

43. one reason that people over the age of 65 should not have their driver's licenses cancelled

Explanatory Topics

1. explain "a stitch in time saves nine"
2. explain "if wishes were horses, beggars would ride"
3. explain "it's useless to cry over spilled milk"
4. explain "a penny saved is a penny earned"
5. explain "spare the rod and spoil the child"
6. explain "the apple doesn't fall far from the tree"
7. explain one reason that a car's oil needs to be changed regularly
8. explain the most difficult aspect of being a student
9. explain the most difficult aspect of being under the age of 50
10. explain the most difficult aspect of being over the age of 50
11. explain the major use of the "flea-flicker" play in football
12. explain the most difficult aspect of being the parent of an infant
13. explain the most difficult aspect of being the parent of a child who's between the ages of one and six
14. explain the most difficult aspect of being the parent of a child who's between the ages of six and twelve
15. explain the most difficult aspect of being the parent of a female teenager
16. explain the most difficult aspect of being the parent of a male teenager
17. explain the most rewarding aspect of being the parent of an infant
18. explain the most rewarding aspect of being the parent of a child who's between the ages of one and six
19. explain the most rewarding aspect of being the parent of a child who's between the ages of six and twelve
20. explain the most rewarding aspect of being the parent of a female teenager
21. explain the most rewarding aspect of being the parent of a male teenager
22. explain the most important step in buying a used car
23. explain the most important step in buying a new car
24. explain the most difficult aspect of being the parent of a male who is over the age of 25
25. explain the most rewarding aspect of being the parent of a male who is over the age of 25
26. explain the most difficult aspect of being the parent of a female who is over the age of 25
27. explain the most rewarding aspect of being the parent of a female who is over the age of 25

28. explain the most difficult aspect of being a grandparent

29. explain the most rewarding aspect of being a grandparent

30. explain the most difficult aspect of living next to people who like to give parties

31. explain the most rewarding aspect of living next to people who like to give parties

32. explain what children need most from parents

33. explain what your first program change would be if you were president of a major commercial television network

34. explain the most drastic change in your everyday life if reading were illegal

35. explain the first thing you would do to improve America if you were elected president

36. explain the one element necessary for your happiness—love, friends, success, or something else

37. explain the most important step in being a successful babysitter

38. explain why you wish you had lived a century ago

39. explain why you wish you could be born a century from now

40. explain why you would like to have a telephone that enables the person you're talking with to see you

41. explain why you would not like to have a telephone that enables the person you're talking with to see you

Descriptive Topics

1. describe Rambette

2. describe Peony McAllister

3. describe Mongo

4. describe the relative you are most comfortable with

5. describe the weirdest gift you ever received

6. describe the best boss you've ever had

7. describe the worst boss you've ever had

8. describe your favorite possession

9. describe your favorite breakfast

10. describe your favorite body of water

11. describe your favorite childhood toy

12. describe yourself from your boss's point of view

13. describe yourself from your pet's point of view

14. describe yourself from your favorite relative's point of view

15. describe yourself from your least favorite relative's point of view

16. describe yourself from the point of view of the teacher of your easiest class

17. describe yourself from the point of view of the teacher of your most difficult class
18. describe the relative you are most uncomfortable with
19. describe the one physical characteristic you would change about yourself if you could
20. describe the one character trait you would change about yourself if you could
21. describe your favorite sport
22. describe your favorite hobby
23. describe your favorite person
24. describe the scariest thing you ever saw
25. describe the funniest thing you ever saw
26. describe your least favorite household chore
27. describe your favorite household chore
28. describe yourself from your dentist's point of view
29. describe your least favorite noise
30. describe your least favorite food
31. describe your least favorite television program
32. describe your favorite article of clothing
33. describe your least favorite article of clothing
34. describe your favorite season
35. describe your least favorite season
36. describe your favorite music
37. describe your favorite radio station
38. describe your favorite city
39. describe your favorite place on earth
40. describe the worst experience you ever had on a commercial flight

Narrative Topics

1. tell about a mistake that taught you an important lesson
2. tell about the happiest memory of your childhood
3. tell about your most disappointing Christmas
4. tell about your favorite fantasy
5. tell your side of an argument you had recently
6. tell the other person's side of an argument you had recently
7. tell about your favorite childhood bedtime story
8. tell about your least favorite childhood bedtime story
9. tell about your favorite childhood nursery rhyme

10. tell about your least favorite childhood nursery rhyme

11. tell about your most embarrassing experience

12. tell about your most triumphant experience

13. tell about your favorite year in elementary school

14. tell about your least favorite year in elementary school

15. tell about your favorite subject in elementary school

16. tell about your least favorite subject in elementary school

17. tell about your earliest memory

18. tell about the most interesting thing that happened to you yesterday

19. tell about a time when you were punished for something you didn't do

20. tell about a time when you punished someone unfairly

21. tell about a time when you got credit for something you didn't do

22. tell about a time when you unintentionally got someone into trouble

23. tell about a time when you were blamed for something you didn't do

24. tell about a time when you blamed someone unfairly

25. tell about how you treated your babysitters when you were little

26. tell about how your parents got you to eat vegetables when you were little

27. tell about your first day of school when you were six years old

28. tell about your worst experience with a machine

29. tell about your most satisfying experience with a machine

30. tell about how your parents got you to take medicine when you were little

31. tell about how you learned to swim

32. tell about how you learned to cook

33. tell about how you learned to water-ski

34. tell about how you learned to drive

35. tell about how you learned to jump rope

36. tell about how you learned to iron

37. tell about how you learned to paint a ceiling

38. tell about how you learned to type

39. tell about how you learned to read

40. tell about how you broke a bad habit

WRITING TOPIC SENTENCES

Please look back at the topics you marked—the ones that interested you most. On page 176, write a topic sentence for each of the topics you marked. (Please remember that a topic sentence must be a sentence and must be limited enough to be dealt with adequately in one paragraph.)

1. _____

_____

_____

2. _____

_____

_____

3. _____

_____

_____

4. _____

_____

_____

PRACTICE IN PARAGRAPH DEVELOPMENT

Now look at the four topic sentences you wrote and choose the one that you're proudest of and happiest with. Copy your favorite topic sentence here and, in the space below it, jot down the things that you want to say in your paragraph.

_____

_____

_____

_____

_____

_____

_____

_____

_____

_____

_____

Now look at your list to see if you have left out anything that you wanted to mention. See if you have jotted down something (now that you stop to think about it) that doesn't really belong in your paragraph. Cross it out.

A handy hint for getting started on the first draft of your paragraph is to pretend that you have just met someone at a party; you look him or her right in the eye and say your topic sentence. Your conversational partner would look interested and then would say something like:

"Go on—please tell me more."

"Can you give me some examples?"

"What do you mean?"

Look again at your list of jottings. Have you said anything that you don't need? Have you left out something that you do need? Recopy your list and then put your jottings into sentences. Try to make sure that each sentence leads logically to another until you have fulfilled the promise of your topic sentence. Imagine your conversational partner's face; is there a smile of absolute understanding, is there a look of bewilderment, or are the eyes closed in bored slumber?

POLISHING YOUR PARAGRAPH

Once you have the rough draft written, go back and work on each sentence, polishing it until you're sure that you have used the constructions, words, and punctuation that you need. Then read the entire paragraph aloud to yourself (if you can find a place where people won't think you've lost your mind) to catch some things that perhaps you missed in your haste to get your ideas on paper—spelling, words left out, verb endings, apostrophes, periods or question marks left out, etc.

Then—here comes the hard part—pretend that someone else, maybe someone who is not your favorite person in the universe, has written the paragraph. Would you criticize anything? If so, fix it.

A MINI CHECKLIST FOR YOUR PARAGRAPH

1. Examine your topic sentence carefully; does it arouse expectations that are satisfied by the rest of the paragraph?

2. Does sentence 2 relate to sentence 1? Does sentence 3 relate to sentences 2 and 1? Check the relationship of each sentence to the one that goes before it and to the topic sentence.

3. Have you given enough supporting details to support your topic sentence?

4. Is each sentence grammatically correct?

5. Is each sentence absolutely clear?

6. Is each sentence free of unnecessary repetition and of unnecessary words?

7. If spelling is not your major skill, have you checked doubtful words with a dictionary?

8. Have you proofread carefully? (Reading the entire paragraph backwards will force your eyes and your mind to focus on each individual word. This sounds crazy, but it works!)

9. Have you read your paragraph aloud at least once?

10. Are you happy with your concluding sentence? Does it bring the entire paragraph to a neat, satisfying close?

A MAXI CHECKLIST FOR PARAGRAPH FINE-TUNING

1. Paragraph is on one of the assigned topics
   Topic sentence properly limited
   Topic sentence indented
   Adequate supporting detail
   Sentence variety
   Meaning of each sentence clear
   Promise of topic sentence fulfilled
   Effective concluding sentence

2. Wordiness
   Wrong word
   Usage
   Needless repetition
   Irrelevant material
   Carelessness (words left out, words written twice, missing letters, etc.)

3. Incomplete sentence:
   no subject
   no verb
   dependent clause
   participial phrase
   Commas before a conjunction joining independent clauses (Rule 1)
   Commas separating items in a series (Rule 2)
   Comma after an introductory dependent clause (Rule 3)
   Semicolon joining independent clauses (Rule 13)
   Proper end punctuation
   Unnecessary commas
   Subject–verb agreement
   Appropriate tense
   Consistent tense
   Correct form of irregular verbs
   No active–passive switches
   Pronoun reference
   Pronoun case
   Correct formation of plurals
   Correct formation of possessives
   Correct formation of contractions
   Double negative

4. Homophones
    to   too
    its   it's
    your   you're
    their   they're   there
    whose   who's
    Spelling
    Unnecessary abbreviation

WRITING ANOTHER PARAGRAPH

Please look back at page 176 and select another of the topic sentences you wrote. Follow the same steps as you did for your first paragraph.

1. Write down the things you want to be sure to include in your paragraph.

2. Pretend that you are actually talking to someone about your topic; better yet, find a real person to discuss your topic with.

3. Add to your jottings those details that you know a conversational partner would ask for.

4. Examine your list of jottings carefully and cross out anything that now strikes you as irrelevant.

5. Translate your jottings into sentences.

6. Work on a snappy concluding sentence.

7. Polish each sentence until it says exactly what you want it to say.

8. Apply the Mini Checklist; tinker with anything that needs it.

9. Apply the Maxi Checklist; tinker again.

10. Relax and be proud of yourself and of your paragraph.

Now do the same for the other two topic sentences you wrote on page 176.

WRITING A TWO-PARAGRAPH PAPER

Now that you are experienced in writing single, self-contained paragraphs, you can tackle a bit more. Look back at the lists of paragraph topics on pages 170 through 175. You'll notice that, particularly in the Persuasive and Explanatory lists, some topics logically go together; for example, an advantage of owning a pet and a disadvantage of owning a pet could each be treated in a separate paragraph, but the paragraphs would be closely related—you'd be examining both sides of the topic of pet ownership.

Two paragraphs will give you a little more room for a slightly less limited topic than the single, self-contained paragraph allows. Your second paragraph, though closely related to the first, lets you pick up a new line of thought. The procedure for writing a multiparagraph essay is essentially the same as the one you have grown to love:

> topic sentence
>
> jottings—zero draft
>
> imaginary (or real) conversation about the topic
>
> more jottings
>
> jottings into sentences
>
> refinement of sentences
>
> Mini and Maxi Checklists
>
> final polishing of paragraph

You can save your snappy concluding sentence for the last one in the paper, so the reader will know that he has come to the end of a thoroughly satisfying two-paragraph piece of writing.

TRANSITIONS

Links between sentences in a paragraph and between paragraphs are called **transitions** (from Latin words that mean *going across*). Transitions make your writing flow smoothly and logically, so your readers don't have to work too hard to understand what you mean. If you make your readers work too hard, you'll lose them. Good, clear writing is a demonstration of courtesy and consideration for your readers. You are asking them to follow your line of thought and to agree with you; any irritants, sloppiness, or lack of consideration for them will make them want to stop reading. They can't read your mind, so they need your basic thought, supported by specific examples of exactly what you mean, presented in the clearest possible terms. Transitions help by linking ideas in a logical way.

Here are some handy transitional words and phrases that express certain relationships between sentences and between paragraphs:

However means that you're about to insert an opposing aspect.
Similarly means that a comparison is coming.
On the other hand means that a contrast is on the way.
For example or **for instance** introduces a specific example.
As a result means that you're going to state the consequences of previous statements.
Moreover means that you're going to add more fuel to your argument.
All in all or **therefore** or **thus** prepares the reader for a conclusion.

Here are some more handy transitional devices:

First (not first*ly*) means that the statement starts a list of major points.
Second (not second*ly*) progresses logically from **first.**
Third (not third*ly*) progresses logically from **second.**

Finally or **last** concludes the list of major points you want to make.

This or **these** or **those** guides the reader without having to repeat everything: **these** facts show; **this** problem persists.

A PARTICULARLY HANDY DEVICE FOR MOVING FROM ONE PARAGRAPH TO THE NEXT

The only slightly tricky aspect of a multiparagraph piece is getting smoothly from one paragraph to the next. One especially effective way of doing this is to repeat the last word of the preceding paragraph in the first sentence of the next paragraph.

Suppose we are writing a two-paragraph essay about some of the problems of America's poor:

America's poor have problems that need immediate attention. _____

_____

_____ (imagine that these lines are filled with seven or eight sentences of magnificent supporting detail) _____

_____

_____ . These problems need immediate **solutions.** (last sentence of paragraph 1)

There are three obvious **solutions** *to the problems of America's poor.* _____

_____

_____

_____ (imagine that these lines are filled with

seven or eight sentences of magnificent supporting detail, too) _____

_____ .

(snappy concluding sentence here)

Do you see how easily the repetition of *solutions* got us from the first paragraph to the second?

Writing Assignments

Select one topic from the following list and write two clear, related paragraphs about it. Please underline the topic sentence of each paragraph and give your composition a title. (One-paragraph compositions don't really need titles because a quick glance at the topic sentence will let the reader know what the paragraph's about, but it's courteous to provide an informative or attention-getting title for pieces that are longer than one paragraph.)

Persuasive Topics

1. an advantage of owning a pet/a disadvantage of owning a pet
2. an advantage of owning your home/a disadvantage of owning your home
3. an advantage of renting your home/a disadvantage of renting your home
4. an advantage of being part of a large family/a disadvantage of being part of a large family
5. one reason that people should have to retire at the age of 50/one reason that people should not have to retire at the age of 50
6. an advantage of a college education/a disadvantage of a college education
7. one reason that elementary school should be in session all year, including the summer/one reason that elementary school should not be in session all year
8. one reason that the voting age should be raised to 25/one reason that the voting age should not be raised to 25
9. one reason that tobacco advertising should be forbidden in the United States/one reason that tobacco advertising should not be forbidden in the United States
10. one reason that every business establishment that has 15 or more employees should have a child-care facility on the premises/one reason that every business establishment that has 15 or more employees should not have a child-care facility on the premises
11. one advantage of being female at the end of the twentieth century/one disadvantage of being female at the end of the twentieth century
12. one advantage of being male at the end of the twentieth century/one disadvantage of being male at the end of the twentieth century
13. one advantage of living in a small town/one disadvantage of living in a small town
14. one advantage of living in a city/one disadvantage of living in a city
15. one reason that police officers should use tranquilizer pellets instead of bullets/one reason that police officers should not use tranquilizer pellets instead of bullets
16. one reason that school children should be bused to achieve racial integration/one reason that school children should not be bused to achieve racial integration
17. one reason that going to a theater to see a movie is more fun than watching a video of the movie at home/one reason that watching a video of a movie at home is more fun than going to a theater to see the movie
18. one reason that people over the age of 65 should have their driver's licenses cancelled/one reason that people over the age of 65 should not have their driver's licenses cancelled

Select one topic from the following list and write two clear, related paragraphs about it. Underline the topic sentence of each paragraph and give your composition a title.

Explanatory Topics

1. explain the most difficult aspect of being under the age of 50/the most difficult aspect of being over the age of 50

2. explain the most difficult aspect of being the parent of an infant/the most rewarding aspect of being the parent of an infant

3. explain the most difficult aspect of being the parent of a child who's between the ages of one and six/the most rewarding aspect of being the parent of a child who's between the ages of one and six

4. explain the most difficult aspect of being the parent of a child who's between the ages of 6 and 12/the most rewarding aspect of being the parent of a child who's between the ages of 6 and 12

5. explain the most difficult aspect of being the parent of a female teenager/the most rewarding aspect of being the parent of a female teenager

6. explain the most difficult aspect of being the parent of a male teenager/the most rewarding aspect of being the parent of a male teenager

7. explain the most difficult aspect of being the parent of a male who is over the age of 25/the most rewarding aspect of being the parent of a male who is over the age of 25

8. explain the most difficult aspect of being the parent of a female who is over the age of 25/the most rewarding aspect of being the parent of a female who is over the age of 25

9. explain the most difficult aspect of being a grandparent/the most rewarding aspect of being a grandparent

10. explain the most difficult aspect of living next to people who like to give parties/the most rewarding aspect of living next to people who like to give parties

11. explain why you would like to have a telephone that enables the person you're talking with to see you/why you would not like to have a telephone that enables the person you're talking with to see you

Create your own topic and write two clear, related paragraphs about it. Underline the topic sentence of each paragraph and give your composition a title.

A THREE-PARAGRAPH PIECE

Read the following assignments carefully and put a checkmark beside the one you prefer:

1. At home, spend one complete hour blindfolded (preferably when other people are around, so you won't hurt yourself trying to answer the telephone). No peeking! As soon as the hour is over, make notes about your experience. Then write a well-organized, powerful, three-paragraph paper about what being blind was like for you. Your paper should communicate your experience clearly and should make your reader understand exactly

how you felt; specific examples are essential. Underline the topic sentence of each paragraph.

2. Spend some time observing aged people; shopping centers and nursing homes are excellent places for observation. Look at how elderly people move, listen to their way of speaking, watch their facial expressions, and, most important of all, observe the attitudes of the people who are accompanying them. Are their attitudes impatient, kind, rude, or loving? Take notes about what you observe and then write a well-organized powerful, three-paragraph paper about what it would be like to be 83 years old. Your paper should be written from the point of view of an 83-year-old person and should use "I" throughout. Your paper should make your reader understand exactly what being 83 would be like for you; specific examples are essential. Underline the topic sentence of each paragraph.

THESIS STATEMENTS AND ESSAYS

Just as each paragraph needs its own topic sentence to state the main idea of the paragraph, a theme (or an essay) needs a sentence that states the main idea of the entire piece of writing; such a statement is called a **thesis statement.** It usually appears in the first paragraph and may even serve as the topic sentence for that introductory paragraph. As you write your three-paragraph piece, you'll need to keep your thesis statement firmly in mind, so you won't be tempted to stray. On this page, write a thesis statement for the assignment you chose on pages 183 and 184.

_____

_____

_____

Guided by your thesis statement, plan each paragraph with specific details, work on each sentence, pay especially careful attention to transitions, check the Mini and Maxi Checklists, make sure that your concluding sentence is all that you want it to be, and you will have written an **essay.** The word might be a little frightening until you realize that it's merely a short composition on a single subject, usually presenting the personal views of the author. Essays are made of paragraphs, which are made of sentences, which are made of words; you're thoroughly familiar with all the components of an essay, so fear not!

MORE WRITING PRACTICE

From the following topics, choose the one in each category that interests you most. This time, you aren't limited to just one advantage, disadvantage, reason, or aspect. You may include as many as you wish.

Persuasive Topics

1. the advantages and disadvantages of owning a pet
2. the advantages and disadvantages of homeownership
3. the advantages and disadvantages of renting a home
4. an advantage and a disadvantage of being part of a large family
5. reasons for and against mandatory retirement at the age of 50
6. the advantages and disadvantages of a college education
7. why elementary schools should be in session all year
8. why elementary schools should not be in session all year
9. why the voting age should be raised to 25
10. why the voting age should not be raised to 25
11. why tobacco advertising should be forbidden in the United States
12. why tobacco advertising should not be forbidden in the United States
13. why every business establishment that has fifteen or more employees should have a child-care facility on the premises
14. why every business establishment that has fifteen or more employees should not have a child-care facility on the premises
15. why the end of the twentieth century is a good time to be female
16. why the end of the twentieth century is not a good time to be female
17. why the end of the twentieth century is a good time to be male
18. why the end of the twentieth century is not a good time to be male
19. why living in a small town is better than living in a city
20. why living in a city is better than living in a small town
21. why police officers should use tranquilizer pellets instead of bullets
22. why police officers should not use tranquilizer pellets instead of bullets
23. why school children should be bused to achieve racial integration
24. why school children should not be bused to achieve racial integration
25. why going to a movie theater is more fun than watching a home video
26. why watching a home video is more fun than going to a movie theater
27. why people over the age of 65 should have their driver's licenses cancelled
28. why people over the age of 65 should not have their driver's licenses cancelled

Explanatory Topics

1. the difficulties of being under the age of 50
2. the difficulties of being over the age of 50
3. the difficulties of being the parent of an infant
4. the rewards of being the parent of an infant

5. the difficulties of being the parent of a child who's between the ages of one and six

6. the rewards of being the parent of a child who's between the ages of one and six

7. the difficulties of being the parent of a child who's between the ages of 6 and 12

8. the rewards of being the parent of a child who's between the ages of 6 and 12

9. the difficulties of being the parent of a female teenager

10. the rewards of being the parent of a female teenager

11. the difficulties of being the parent of a male teenager

12. the rewards of being the parent of a male teenager

13. the difficulties of being the parent of a male who's over the age of 25

14. the rewards of being the parent of a male who's over the age of 25

15. the difficulties of being the parent of a female who's over the age of 25

16. the rewards of being the parent of a female who is over the age of 25

17. the difficulties of being a grandparent

18. the rewards of being a grandparent

19. the difficulties of living next to people who like to give parties

20. the rewards of living next to people who like to give parties

21. why you want "phone-vision"

22. why you don't want "phone-vision"

Comparison-Contrast Topics

Comparison explains similarities; contrast explains differences. A comparison-contrast essay involves elements of explanation, description, and narration.

1. compare and contrast the best and worst bosses you've ever had

2. compare and contrast your favorite and least favorite relatives

3. compare and contrast your favorite and least favorite seasons

4. compare and contrast your favorite and least favorite vacations

5. compare and contrast your favorite and least favorite holidays

6. compare and contrast your favorite and least favorite modes of transportation

7. compare and contrast your favorite and least favorite articles of clothing

8. compare and contrast your favorite and least favorite types of music

9. compare and contrast your favorite and least favorite classes

10. compare and contrast your favorite and least favorite magazines

11. compare and contrast your favorite and least favorite cities

12. compare and contrast the best and worst meals you've ever had

13. compare and contrast your favorite and least favorite household chores

14. compare and contrast the best and worst days of your life so far

15. compare and contrast your tenth birthday and your sixteenth birthday

Write thesis statements for each of the three topics you have chosen.

1. _____

_____

_____

2. _____

_____

_____

3. _____

_____

_____

Now choose the one thesis statement that you'd like to develop into an essay and go to it!

MORE IDEAS FOR WRITING

Writing is a useful tool for examining all aspects of yourself and of your personal world. It can help you examine and interpret your immediate experience thoughtfully and patiently. Writing is a way of dealing with life; it is not something that is done just in the classroom; it is not something that insists on mechanical correctness above all (the more you know about how to use your language, the less you'll be confined by worrying about whether you're using it correctly, and the more able you'll feel to express your thoughts and feelings). It is, ideally, an essential part of everyday life—as important for psychological health as nutritious meals are to physical health. Writing is a way to gain wisdom about life.

Here are some writing topics for your private use.

1. Describe an argument you recently had with someone you love. What did it feel like to know you were right? Why did the other person believe that he or she was right? What did the experience teach you about yourself and about the person you argued with?

2. Write a letter to someone who has upset you, and use the liveliest words you know. You needn't actually send the letter; you might decide to rip it to shreds and eat the pieces, but you'll feel better once your feelings are on paper.

3. Write a letter to yourself in which you discuss your admirable qualities.

4. Write a letter to yourself in which you discuss your not-so-admirable qualities.

5. Describe, from start to finish, a day that would be perfect for you: where you'd be living, with whom, what kind of job and family you'd have. End your composition with information about what you're actually doing to make your perfect day a reality someday.

6. Write a letter to your child, praising some particular behavior or character trait, giving specific examples of the praiseworthy event and telling how you feel about it. Slip the letter under the child's pillow. (Sort of like a cash-poor Tooth Fairy!)

7. Write a letter to your child, inquiring about some misbehavior that occurred recently and telling how you feel about it. Slip the letter under the door of the child's room. Invite the child to respond in writing, and promise not to pay attention to spelling and punctuation.

8. Write about some or all of the following:

joy	stress
fun	loyalty
love	generosity
laughter	rejection
pain	hands
death	faces
anxiety	

Glossary of Terms

including definitions, observations, and assorted bits of advice

action verb An action verb, as opposed to a linking verb, can be described by an adverb. A few verbs are sometimes action and sometimes linking verbs: *to taste, to sound, to smell, to feel, to look, to become,* and *to remain.*

adjective An adjective describes a noun or a pronoun by giving information about it, such as how many, what size, what color, etc: "The *six small, squeaky* squidlets ate the *rubber* ducky." Adjectives have three degrees of comparison: the positive, comparative, and superlative. Proper adjectives are formed from proper nouns, and they are always capitalized: *Italian* shoes, *Swiss* watches, and *African* art.

adjective clause An adjective clause is a dependent clause functioning as an adjec-

tive: "The man *who came to dinner* didn't help wash the dishes."

adverb Adverbs describe verbs, adjectives, and other adverbs: "He waltzes *weirdly.*" "She is *rather* raucous." "It lurks *too listlessly.*" Adverbs usually answer such questions as *when, where, how,* or *to what extent.* Adverbs have three degrees of comparison: the positive, comparative, and superlative.

adverb clause An adverb clause is a dependent clause functioning as an adverb: "They laughed *when I sat down at the electric kazoo.*"

antecedent A handy word to use when you're talking about pronouns: a pronoun's antecedent is the word or group of words the pronoun is replacing. This is known as

pronoun reference. "Mongo didn't clean his room; he is in a lot of trouble." (*He* is replacing *Mongo,* so *Mongo* is the antecedent of the pronoun *he.*) If a pronoun's antecedent is singular, the pronoun must be singular; if a pronoun's antecedent is plural, the pronoun must be plural. This is known as **pronoun agreement.**

apostrophe An apostrophe indicates the possessive form of nouns, appears in contractions, and, with *s,* is used to form the plural of letters of the alphabet, numbers, symbols, and words referred to as words.

appositive A word or group of words that can take the place of the noun that comes right before it. Appositives can be restrictive or nonrestrictive: "My sister *Barbara* makes the world's best chocolate cake"; "My mother, *a member of the Loyal Temperance Legion,* drinks nothing stronger than cranberry juice."

article Although *a, an,* and *the* are adjectives, they are usually called articles; *the* is a **definite article,** specifying a particular item: "*The* old gray mare in no way resembles her former self." *A* and *an* are **indefinite articles,** and they don't specify particular items: "A man, a plan, a canal, an argument." *An* is used before words beginning with a vowel sound.

auxiliary verbs Also known as **helping verbs,** auxiliary verbs help in the formation of tenses and of the passive voice. The past participle and the present participle of a verb cannot function as verbs without help from an auxiliary. Some popular auxiliary verbs are *am, are, is, was, were, have, has, had, do, does, did, may, might, could, would, should, can,* and *will.*

basic sentence pattern Beware of using the basic sentence pattern (subject–verb–object) all the time, because your readers will fall asleep from boredom and crash to the floor in a stupor.

clause A group of words containing both a subject and a whole verb. An **independent clause** can also be called a **main clause** or a **sentence**—it can stand alone and make sense. A **dependent clause,** also known as a **subordinate clause,** depends on more information to make it complete; a dependent clause begins with a signal word (subordinating conjunction). The three major clauses are independent, dependent, and Santa.

cliché (pronounced klee-SHAY) An expression that has been repeated so often that it no longer provides a fresh, new way of saying something: "*Last but not least, you'll pass this course with flying colors, or I'll eat my hat.*"

colon The colon (:) introduces an explanation, an example, or a list of items.

comma A courteous, clarifying punctuation mark (,) that keeps your readers from pulling their hair out in wild confusion and frustration.

comma splice The result of trying to use a mere comma without a coordinating conjunction to join sentences.

comparative degree The comparative degree of an adjective or adverb is used for comparisons between two items. Strawberries are *smaller* than basketballs.

complete subject The complete subject of a clause includes everything that goes along with the noun or pronoun that drives the verb.

complex sentence A sentence with at least one independent clause and one dependent clause: "*I'm lucky because you're wonderful.*"

compound-complex sentence A sentence with at least two independent clauses and at least one dependent clause: "*I'm lucky because you're wonderful, but I carry a four-leaf clover, too.*"

compound predicate More than one verb with the same subject in a clause: "Fedonia *coughed, sneezed, and sniffled through-out the service."*

compound sentence A sentence with at least two independent clauses: *"You're won-derful, and I'm lucky."*

compound subject More than one subject of a verb in a clause: *"Thomasina, Ri-charda, and Harriet celebrate Martin Van Buren's birthday with fireworks."*

concluding sentence of a paragraph A sen-tence that brings the development of the paragraph's topic sentence to a satisfying close.

conjugation Taking a verb through all the forms it can have in a certain tense.

conjunction A joiner of words, phrases, clauses, or sentences.

conjunctive adverb An adverb that indicates a very strong relationship between two independent clauses and that functions as a joiner; some of the most-used ones include: *therefore, however, indeed, otherwise.*

consonant The letters of the alphabet except *a, e, i, o,* and *u,* which are vowels.

contraction A short way of saying or writing something. In written contractions, an apostrophe shows that some letters and/ or spaces have been omitted. *"You've* been a good friend; he *hasn't."*

contrary-to-fact subjunctive A form of the verb that lets you know that something isn't factual: "If Mongo *were* here, I'd hug him hard."

coordinating conjunction The coordinating conjunctions *and, but, or, nor, for, yet,* and *so* join words, phrases, or clauses of equal weight.

dangling participle The construction that re-sults when an introductory participial phrase doesn't sensibly describe the sub-ject of a sentence: *"Going to sleep,* scary noises filled the room."

dash A dash (—) indicates a sudden break in

thought or a summing up. A dash is two hyphens long: in handwriting, it's a con-tinuous line; on a typewriter, it's two hy-phens with no space between and no space separating it from the words before and after it.

definite article *The* is a definite article, spec-ifying a particular item: *"The* old gray mare in no way resembles her former self."

demonstrative pronoun *This, that, these,* and *those* are pronouns that point out (demonstrate) a specific noun. "Mongo cleaned his room; *that* is surprising."

dependent clause A group of words contain-ing both a subject and a whole verb but not expressing a complete thought. Also known as a **subordinate clause,** it de-pends on more information to make it complete. A dependent clause begins with a signal word (subordinating conjunction) or a relative pronoun.

direct object A noun or a pronoun that re-ceives the action of a verb: "Rambette ate the *blowtorch."*

direct quotation Enclosed in quotation marks, the exact words of a speaker or writer.

double comparison A comparison in which the degree of the adjective or adverb is formed twice by adding *er* or *est* and using *more* and *most:* "You are *more* friendl*ier* than your sister"; "You're the *most* friend-l*iest* person I know."

double negative Two negatives in the same clause that cancel each other out, so the clause ends up meaning the opposite of what the writer intends: "I haven*'t never* seen a purple cow." = "I have seen a pur-ple cow."

English teacher A blessed creature who is a candidate for sainthood.

equal adjectives Adjectives that describe the same noun; their positions are inter-changeable: "The *wild, woolly* wombats jumped on the *tired, unhappy* earth-worms."

essay   A short composition on a single subject, usually presenting the personal views of the author.

exclamation   A word that simply expresses emotion; it has no grammatical relationship with the rest of the sentence. Any word that's said with enough oomph can be an exclamation: "*Spaghetti and petunias!*" "*Wombats on a wagon!*" "*Fluorescent photo opportunities!*" *Yes, no, well,* and *oh* are mild exclamations, and they are usually followed by a comma when they appear at the beginning of a sentence.

figurative language   As opposed to literal language, which is no-frills, no-nonsense factual, figurative language employs figures of speech for dramatic effect.

figure of speech   An expression that aims for a forceful, dramatic image, so your readers will see, hear, taste, touch, smell, and experience things exactly as you want them to. Some popular figures of speech are the **simile,** the **metaphor,** the **hyperbole,** and **personification.**

finite verb   A verb with definite person, number, and tense that can function as the main verb of a clause; finite verbs can also be called **whole verbs** (although I think I'm alone, so far, in preferring to call them that).

fused sentence   Another name for a *run-on sentence.*

gerund   A verb's present participle (the *ing* one) functioning as a noun. Use the possessive form of a noun or pronoun that comes immediately before a gerund. "*Your weeping* is making my pancakes soggy."

helping verb   Also known as **auxiliary verbs,** helping verbs help in the formation of tenses and of the passive voice. The past participle and the present participle of a verb cannot function as verbs without aid from

a helper. Some popular helping verbs are *am, are, is, was, were, have, has, had, do, does, did, may, might, could, would, should, can,* and *will.*

homophone   A word that sounds exactly like another word but that is very different when it is written and in its meaning: *it's, its; you're, your; they're, their, there; who's, whose; to, too.*

hyperbole (pronounced high-PER-bo-lee)   Extravagant exaggeration: "*I'm so tired I could sleep on a barbed-wire fence.*"

hypercorrection   A grammatical fault that results when people automatically use an adverb with a verb without thinking about the distinction between action verbs and linking verbs. "The frying bacon smells *wonderfully.*"

hyphen   Use a hyphen (-) to link words for clarity, when you're spelling out a number between twenty and one hundred, and when you run out of room at the end of a line and need to continue a word on the next line.

imperative mood   A verb's mood that expresses a command.

incomplete comparison   Omission of the object of comparison when using the comparative or superlative degree of an adjective or adverb. Something like this will drive your readers right smack up the wall: "*Yogurt is smoother.*" (Smoother than what—a spoonful of gravel?)

incomplete sentence   A group of words that begins with a capital letter and ends with a period or other end punctuation but that is missing either a subject, a whole verb, or the expression of a complete thought. An incomplete sentence is sometimes called a **sentence fragment.**

indefinite article   *A* and *an* are **indefinite articles,** and they don't specify particular items: "*A man, a plan, a canal, an argument.*" *An* is used before words beginning with a vowel sound.

indefinite pronoun *Each, one, none, all, anybody, anyone, somebody, someone, nobody, no one,* and *some* are pronouns that don't replace a specific noun. "Is *anybody* home?"

independent clause A group of words containing both a subject and a whole verb. An independent clause can also be called a **main clause** or a **sentence**—it can stand alone and express a complete thought.

indicative mood A verb's mood that indicates a statement of fact or a question.

indirect object A noun or a pronoun that shows to whom or for whom the action of a verb is done: "The blowtorch gave *Rambette* terrible heartburn."

indirect quotation Not enclosed in quotation marks, an indirect quotation reports what someone said or wrote, but it doesn't use the person's exact words: "Mongo said *that his wombat has warts.*" The direct-quotation version of this would be: "Mongo said, '*My wombat has warts.*'"

infinitive The **infinitive** gets its name because it doesn't have any boundaries of person, number, or tense. The infinitive is a verb's official name; the first word is always *to.*

intransitive verb An intransitive verb doesn't need a direct object to complete its meaning.

irregular verb An irregular verb is one whose simple past tense and past participle are not formed merely by adding *d* or *ed.*

linking verb A linking verb (also known as a **state of being verb),** as opposed to an action verb, merely links the subject of a sentence with more information about the subject and is never described by an adverb. The verb *to be* (in all its forms) is the only verb in English that is always a linking verb and never an action verb.

literal language No-frills, no-nonsense, no-figure-of-speech, factual language.

lively verb A verb that has zing and pizzazz;

it tells the reader how the subject looks, sounds, or acts.

main clause Another name for an independent clause in a complex or compound-complex sentence.

mechanical accuracy In writing, having all components correct—commas where they are needed, verbs in the proper form, clear pronoun reference—everything from sections 3 and 4 of the Maxi Checklist for Paragraph Fine-Tuning (pages 178–179). Mechanical accuracy doesn't guarantee terrific writing, though; that's where sections 1 and 2 of the Maxi Checklist come in. Mastering the mechanics of the language will free your mind to concentrate your energies on *what* you're saying instead of *how* you're saying it.

mental doodling An important first step in the writing process when you get your thoughts about a topic to move through your arm and onto the paper. Mental doodles turn into your **zero draft** as soon as they hit paper (or sand, dust, tablecloths—anything that can be written in or on).

metaphor (pronounced MET-ah-four): A figure of speech that equates essentially unlike things: "*This classroom is a zoo.*"

misplaced modifiers Adjectives and adverbs (or phrases and clauses functioning as adjectives and adverbs) that are not positioned clearly next to the words they're describing; misplaced modifiers are a primary cause of hair-hurting, teeth-gnashing confusion for your readers.

mixed metaphor A bizarre, confusing construction that results when writers lose track of the qualities and characteristics of the metaphors they're using in their writing: "*The candidate changed horses in mid-stream and threw the baby out with the bathwater.*"

modifiers Adjectives and adverbs (or phrases

and clauses functioning as adjectives and adverbs).

mood   A verb form that indicates the attitude of the speaker or writer toward the action or condition expressed. The **indicative mood** is used for statements of fact and for questions; the **imperative mood** is used for commands, and the **subjunctive mood** is used to indicate doubt, wishes, or statements that are contrary to fact.

nonrestrictive element   A word, phrase, or clause that contains information that is *not* essential to the meaning of a sentence: "My dog, *whose name is Barkus*, has fleas."

noun   A **common noun** names a person, place, thing, relationship, concept, or idea: *wombats, week, bumper*. A **proper noun** is the name of a specific person, place, thing, language, country, day, month, or religion: *Peony McAllister, Spanish, Australia, Tuesday, August, Methodism*. Proper nouns are always capitalized, no matter where they appear in a sentence.

noun clause   A dependent clause functioning as a noun: "*Whoever volunteers to follow the elephants in the parade* is brave."

number   singular or **plural** (when used to identify forms of nouns, pronouns, and verbs)

object   A noun or pronoun whose form is affected by a verb or a preposition. A **direct object** receives the action of a verb; an **indirect object** shows to whom or for whom the action of a verb is done; the **object of a preposition** follows a preposition.

object personal pronoun   A pronoun used as a direct object, as an indirect object, or as the object of a preposition: *me, you, him, her, it, us, them*.

only   As far as precise placement is concerned, one of the trickiest four-letter words in the language.

paragraph   A unit of composition that is made up of related sentences in logical order that develop one main idea.

parallelism (or **parallel structure**)   Words, phrases, or clauses of the same grammatical kind in a pair or in a series: "Scouts are *brave, clean,* and *reverent*"; "Mongo likes *snakes, snails,* and *worms*."

parentheses   Use parentheses ( ) around words or groups of words that give explanatory, by-the-way information that is not absolutely essential to the meaning of the sentence.

participial phrase   A group of words containing a participle; a participial phrase that comes first in a sentence must describe the subject of the sentence.

participle   Only *part* of a verb; the past participle and the present participle must be helped by an auxiliary verb in order to function as verbs. Without an auxiliary, the past participle becomes an adjective; without an auxiliary, the present participle (the *ing* one) becomes either a noun or an adjective.

passive voice   A verb is in the passive voice when the subject is receiving the action: "The frog **was kissed** by the princess." *Was kissed* is in the passive voice here; the subject of the sentence is *frog*, and it is being acted upon. (The performer of the action is tucked away in the prepositional phrase *by the princess*.) The passive voice is formed by using the past participle of the verb with some form of the verb *to be*. Only transitive verbs can be put into the passive voice.

person   The form of a pronoun or verb that distinguishes among the speaker or writer (*I, we*), the person or persons being spoken or written to (*you*), and the person, persons, or items that are being spoken about (*he, she, it, they*).

personification   A figure of speech in which objects and ideas behave in human ways:

"The rock squatted stubbornly in the middle of the road and refused to budge."

phrase   A group of related words that acts as a single part of speech and that lacks a subject (a noun or pronoun about which something is being said), or a whole verb (one with person, number, and tense), or both. For example, *dancing in the moonlight* is a phrase; there is no subject, nor is there a whole verb—*dancing* is only part of a verb, so it must have help if it's going to do the work of a verb.

pluperfect   Another name for the past perfect tense.

plural   A noun or a pronoun is plural when it refers to *more than one* person or item.

plural possessive   To form the plural possessive of a noun, first form the plural; if the plural form ends in s, merely add an apostrophe after the s; if the plural does not end in s, add an 's to form the plural possessive.

positive degree   The positive degree of an adjective or adverb is just the plain adjective or adverb.

possessive   A form of a noun or pronoun that indicates ownership.

possessive personal pronoun   A personal pronoun (*I, you, he, she, it, we, they*) in the possessive form: *my, mine; your, yours; his; her, hers; its; our, ours; their, theirs.* No apostrophes appear in the possessive form of personal pronouns.

predicate   The part of the sentence that isn't the complete subject. The **simple predicate** of a clause is just the whole verb; the **complete predicate** is everything that's left over after you identify the complete subject.

predicate adjective   An adjective that follows a linking verb: "I am *ecstatic.*"

preposition   A word that shows the relation of a noun or pronoun to some other word in the sentence: "I am running *over, under, around,* and *through* the laundry."

prepositional phrase   A group of words that begins with a preposition and ends with a noun or pronoun: *in the kitchen, beyond the sunset, over the hill, without us.* Prepositional phrases often function as adverbs, telling us when, where, how, and so on.

principal parts of verbs   A verb has four principal parts: the root form, the simple past, the past participle, and the present participle (the *ing* one).

pronoun   A word that can take the place of a noun: "George and Martha are heading for the cherry tree; please stop *them.*"

   demonstrative pronouns   *This, that, these, those*

   indefinite pronouns   *each, one, none, all, anybody, anyone, somebody, someone, nobody, no one, some*

   personal pronouns   *I, you, he, she, it, they, me, you, him, her, it, us, them*

   reflexive pronouns   *myself, yourself, himself, herself, itself, ourselves, yourselves, themselves*

   relative pronouns   *who, which, that*

pronoun agreement   Agreement in number and gender of a pronoun with its antecedent: if a pronoun's antecedent is singular, the pronoun must be singular; if a pronoun's antecedent is plural, the pronoun must be plural.

pronoun reference   Use of a pronoun to replace a word or group of words (its antecedent): "**Mongo** didn't clean his room; **he** is in a lot of trouble." (*He* is replacing *Mongo,* which is its antecedent.)

proper adjective   Proper adjectives are formed from proper nouns, and they are always capitalized: *Italian* shoes, *Swiss* watches, and *African* art.

proper noun   A proper noun is the name of a specific person, place, thing, language, country, day, month, or religion: *Peony McAllister, Spanish, Australia, Tuesday, August, Methodism.* No matter where they appear in a sentence, proper nouns are always capitalized.

punctuation   The written form of good manners.

quotation marks   Use quotation marks (" ") around the exact words of a speaker and around the titles of book chapters, magazine articles, poems, episodes of television and radio programs, short stories, and songs.

redundancy   Using words that say exactly the same thing, which wastes your readers' time and, sometimes, even insults them: "*In my opinion, I think* that the problem will be *magnified and appear larger* by 7 A.M. *in the morning.*"

reflexive pronoun   *Myself, yourself, himself, herself, itself, ourselves, yourselves,* and *themselves;* they indicate that the subject and object are the same. Reflective pronouns are never used as subjects; they are very useful for emphasis.

regular verb   A verb whose simple past tense and past participle are formed merely by adding *d* (if the root ends in *e*) or *ed;* the simple past form and the past participle of a regular verb are identical.

relative pronoun   Relative pronouns—*who, whoever, whatever, whose, whomever, which, whom, what,* and *that*—can introduce dependent clauses: "Mom's going to make cookies for the first kid *who sweeps out the stables.*" Relative pronouns can also serve as subjects of independent clauses: "*Who* was that masked man?"

restrictive element   A word, phrase, or clause that contains information absolutely essential to the meaning of a sentence: "A cat *who never purrs* is a sour puss."

root   To identify the root (or **basic**) form of a verb, just remove the *to* from the infinitive;

you can then use the root to make other forms of the verb.

run-on sentence   A run-on sentence (also known as a **fused sentence**) has no punctuation at all between two or more independent clauses, which can drive your readers wild with frustration and confusion.

semicolon   A semicolon is stronger than a comma and weaker than a period; use a semicolon to join two related, complete sentences when there is no coordinating conjunction and to separate items in a series when the items already contain commas.

sentence-combining   Combining short, choppy sentences into longer, more interesting ones.

sentence fragment   A group of words that begins with a capital letter and ends with a period or other end punctuation but that is missing either a subject, a whole verb, or the expression of a complete thought. An **incomplete sentence** is sometimes called a sentence fragment.

series   Three or more words, phrases, or clauses in a sentence. Items in a series are separated by commas: "The hockey player *sharpened his skates, powdered his stick,* and *ate the puck.*" If the items already contain commas, separate them with semicolons.

signal word   A subordinating conjunction (*while, when, before, because,* etc.) that begins a dependent clause.

simile   (pronounced SIM-ill-lee) A figure of speech that usually begins with the words *like* or *as,* comparing essentially different things: "This pot roast is *as tough as a boiled owl.*"

simple predicate   Just the stark-naked verb.

simple sentence   A sentence with just one independent clause: "*You're wonderful.*"

simple subject Just the stark-naked noun or pronoun (with no adjectives or frills) that drives the verb.

single quotation marks Use single quotation marks around a direct quotation within a direct quotation.

singular A noun or a pronoun is singular when it refers to *one* person or item.

singular possessive To form the possessive of a singular noun, simply add *an apostrophe* (') *and* s.

state-of-being verb A state-of-being verb (also known as a **linking verb),** as opposed to an action verb, links the subject of a sentence to an adjective or to a noun and is never described by an adverb. The verb *to be* (in all its forms) is the only verb in English that is always a state-of-being verb and never an action verb.

subject A noun or pronoun about which something is being said. In sentences with active verbs, the subject is the actor; in sentences with passive verbs, the subject is usually tucked away in a prepositional phrase.

subject personal pronouns *I, you, he, she, it, we,* and *they* are pronouns used as the subject of a clause.

subject–verb agreement A verb must agree in person and number with its subject; a plural subject requires a verb in the plural form, and a singular subject requires a verb in the singular form.

subjunctive mood A verb's mood that expresses a wish, a possibility, a doubt, or something contrary to fact: "If I *were* you, I'd duck."

subordinate clause Dependent clauses are also known as subordinate clauses because they are less powerful than independent clauses—they are incomplete.

subordinating conjunction A signal word (*while, when, before, because,* etc.) that begins a dependent clause. Subordinating conjunctions join less powerful dependent clauses with independent clauses.

superlative degree The superlative degree of an adjective or adverb is used for comparisons among more than two items: "Amylizzo is the *youngest* of the nine girls in her family."

tense The tense of a verb refers to time.

The **present tense** indicates that the action or state described is taking place now or that it takes place regularly: "I *love* parsnips."

The **simple past tense** indicates that the action or state described both began and ended in the past: "I *had* parsnips for breakfast."

The **future tense** indicates a future action or state: "I **will have** parsnips for a midnight snack."

The **present perfect tense** specifies an action or state that began and ended in the past or that began in the past and continues into the present; it is formed by adding *has* or *have* to the past participle: "I *have enjoyed* parsnips for eight decades."

The **past perfect tense** indicates that the action or state began in the past and ended at some later time in the past. It is formed by adding *had* to the past participle. (Any other verb in the sentence must be in the more recent past than the past perfect.) "I *had* just *finished* my parsnip pudding when the refrigerator exploded."

The **future perfect tense** indicates a future action or state that will be completed at a specific time; it is formed by adding *will have* to the past participle: "Next Tuesday, I *will have eaten* my millionth parsnip."

The **present progressive tense** indicates that the action or state is in progress right now; it is formed with *am, is,* or *are* and the present participle (the *ing* one): "I *am drooling* at the thought of a chocolate-covered parsnip for dessert."

The **past progressive tense** indicates that the action or state was in progress in the past; it is formed with *was* or *were* and the present participle (the *ing* one): "I *was dreaming* of parsnip pancakes when the alarm went off."

The **future progressive tense** indicates that the action or state will be in progress in the future; it is formed with *will be* and the present participle (the *ing* one): "I *will be making* parsnip pies all afternoon."

The **present perfect progressive tense** indicates that the action or state started in the past and is still in progress; it is formed with *has been* or *have been* and the present participle (the *ing* one): "I *have been growing* my own parsnips in flowerpots."

The **past perfect progressive tense** indicates that the action or state began in the past and was in progress until some later time in the past. It is formed by adding *had been* to the present participle (the *ing* one). (Any other verb in the sentence must be in the more recent past than the past perfect progressive.) "I *had been tasting* my parsnip parfait so often while it was cooking yesterday that I lost my appetite for lunch."

The **future perfect progressive tense** indicates that the action or state will be in progress in the future before another time or action takes place. It is formed by adding *will have been* to the present participle (the *ing* one). By the time I get to Phoenix, *you will have been sunbathing* for a week.

that   A useful word for introducing restrictive elements: "Lips *that touch tofu* will never touch mine." It's a bit rude to use *that* with people, though.

thesis statement   A thesis statement is to an essay what a topic sentence is to a paragraph; it states the main idea that the essay will develop.

topic sentence   A general statement that expresses the main idea of a paragraph; the body of the paragraph develops and clarifies the topic sentence by giving supporting details and specific examples.

transitions   Bridges between sentences in a paragraph and between paragraphs; transitions make your writing flow smoothly and logically, so your readers don't have to work too hard to understand what you mean.

transitive verb   A verb is transitive when it needs a direct object (a noun or pronoun that receives the action of the verb) to complete its meaning. Only transitive verbs can be put into the passive voice.

two-way adverbs   Adverbs that are not placed next to the exact words you want them to accompany, so they might go with either of two words.

underlining   Underline titles of books, magazines, plays, movies, and newspapers.

understood subject   When you are issuing commands or making requests, the subject is always understood to be *you*, and it isn't said or written.

verb   A verb indicates action or state of being: "I *dance* at dawn"; "You *are* happy." A whole verb (finite verb) has person, number, and tense and can function as the main verb in a clause.

voice   Verbs have two voices, **active** and **passive.** A verb is in the active voice when the subject is performing the action: "*The princess kissed* the frog." A verb is in the passive voice when the subject is receiving the action: "*The frog was kissed* by the princess." *Was kissed* is in the passive voice here; the subject of the sentence is *frog,* and it is being acted on. (The performer of the action is tucked away in the prepositional phrase *by the princess.)* The passive voice is formed by using the past participle of the verb with some form of the verb *to be.*

vowel   *a, e, i, o,* and *u.* All the other letters of the alphabet are consonants.

which   A useful word for introducing nonrestrictive elements: "Tofu, *which is some people's idea of a gourmet delight,* makes me turn green."

whole verb   A verb with definite person, number, and tense that can function as the main verb of a clause; whole verbs can also be called **finite verbs.**

wordiness   You're guilty of wordiness if you use several words (usually long ones) when a very few words (usually short ones) will convey your meaning more quickly and clearly: "*At this point in time, we are obligated, in a very real sense, to attempt to eschew the employment of our lachrymal glands concerning the descended dairy fluid.*" "*We must now try not to cry over spilled milk.*"

writing   A nifty way of learning about yourself and your world.

zero draft   A stage in the writing process that comes before the rough draft; zero drafts can kick-start your creative process by allowing you to jot down your mental doodlings—every thought that comes into your head about a topic. Because your zero draft is completely private, you can write it on anything with anything.

Punctuation Rules at a Glance

COMMA RULES (,)

1. Use a comma before *and, but, or, nor, for, yet,* and *so* when the word joins two complete sentences.
2. Use a comma to separate items (words, phrases, or clauses) in a series of three or more items.
3. When a dependent clause begins with a subordinating conjunction (*while, when, before, where, unless, after, because, though, wherever, as though, although, as soon as, until, if, once, as if, since, till, as, rather than*), use a comma at the end of the dependent clause if it comes before the independent clause. No comma is needed if the dependent clause comes after the independent clause.
4. Use a comma to separate adjectives that describe the same noun. (These are called **equal adjectives,** and their positions are interchangeable.)
5. Use a pair of commas to set off interrupting words or phrases in a sentence.
6. Use a comma after a participial phrase beginning a sentence.
7. Use a pair of commas to set off nonrestrictive elements in a sentence.

8. Use a comma to set off the names of persons, places, or things being addressed. If the name comes first in a sentence, the comma follows it; if the name comes last, the comma precedes it; if the name appears elsewhere in the sentence, use a comma before and after it.

9. Use a comma to set off short words and phrases, such as *yes, no, well, oh, nevertheless, therefore, after all, finally, in conclusion,* etc., when they appear at the beginning of a sentence.

10. Use a comma with *too* when it means *also* wherever it occurs in a sentence. If *too* comes first, the comma follows it; if *too* comes last, the comma precedes it; if *too* appears elsewhere in the sentence, use a comma before and after it.

11. Use a comma before a conversational question that's added to the end of a statement. (These are questions that are not of life-and-death importance, and the asker usually already knows the answer.)

12. Use a comma to separate words that might be confusing if they were read together. The comma provides a pause for your readers, so they won't have to read the sentence several times to puzzle out what you mean.

SEMICOLON RULES (;)

13. Use a semicolon to join two related complete sentences when there is no conjunction (*and, but, or, nor, for, yet, so*) to join the sentences.

    Some adverbs indicate a very strong relationship between two independent clauses; when they function as joiners, these adverbs are called **conjunctive adverbs**; some of the most-used ones include:

therefore	consequently	besides
moreover	furthermore	in fact
nevertheless	however	indeed
accordingly	likewise	instead
otherwise	thus	still

    Because these conjunctive adverbs mark such a strong relationship between independent clauses, a semicolon must appear between the clauses. If the conjunctive adverb comes first in the second clause, use a comma after the conjunctive adverb (and the semicolon will be before the conjunctive adverb, right between the clauses). If the conjunctive adverb comes last in the second clause, use a comma before it (and the semicolon will remain right between the clauses). If the conjunctive adverb comes elsewhere in the second clause, use a pair of commas around it (and the semicolon will remain right between the clauses).

14. Use a semicolon to separate items in a series when the items already contain commas.

COLON RULE (:)

15. Use a colon to introduce an explanation or an example; it shows that what follows is a fuller explanation of what has been stated.

QUOTATION MARKS (" ")

A. Use quotation marks around the exact words of a speaker (a direct quotation). Use a comma before a direct quotation.

B. Use quotation marks around the titles of book chapters, magazine articles, poems, episodes of television and radio programs, short stories, and songs.

SINGLE QUOTATION MARKS (' ')

Use single quotation marks around a direct quotation within a direct quotation and also around the titles of book chapters, magazine articles, poems, episodes of television and radio programs, short stories, and songs within a direct quotation. (In other words, you can't have double quotation marks within double quotation marks.)

THE HYPHEN (-)

A. Use a hyphen to link words for clarity.

B. Use a hyphen when you're spelling out a number between twenty and one hundred.

C. Use a hyphen when you run out of room at the end of a line and need to continue a word on the next line.

PARENTHESES ( )

Use parentheses around words or groups of words that give explanatory, by-the-way information that is not absolutely essential to the meaning of the sentence.

THE DASH (—)

Use a dash to indicate a sudden break in thought or a summing up.

Exercise Answers

SECTION 1: PARTS OF SPEECH

Nouns (page 2)

Common nouns: ant, cabbage, beauty, cousin, witch, hill, geranium, eraser

Proper nouns (pages 2–3)

1. Bear Paw Pond, Tuesday, October
2. Dr. Seuss, Mulberry Street, Christmas Cove, New Hampshire
3. Rambo Hutchinson, Diet Coke
4. Mr. Smith, Washington, Kalamazoo

Exercise in Common and Proper Nouns (page 3)

1. Fedonia Krump, lady, Pasadena, tea, sympathy
2. Mrs. Johnson, boys, Pete, Repeat
3. Dallas, J. R. Ewing

4. Easter Bunny, eggs, basket, Mike's, bicycle, yolk
5. Venus Flytrap, Grandma's, characters, television
6. Eric, French, toast, fries
7. Dad's, crop, end, July
8. Fred, Wilma, Pebbles, star
9. Mondays, Wednesdays, parking lot, Toyotas, Hondas, Fords
10. Dallas Cowpeople, Superbowl, rodeo, Madison Square Garden, New York City

Pronouns (page 4)

1. it, they
2. she, them, her
3. his, her, she, him, he, his
4. she, her, them
5. he, it, his

Exercise (page 5)

1. you, you'll (this is a contraction for *you will*), us
2. He, his, they, yours
3. their
4. their, them, it, their
5. her, them
6. it, him
7. you, your, I'm (this is a contraction for *I am*), it
8. I, my, my
9. They, their, they're (this is a contraction for *they are*)
10. her, their

Verbs (page 6)

1. complained, dynamited
2. go, buy
3. drove, lost
4. opened, rose, bathed
5. danced, was

Adjectives (page 6)

It was a dark and stormy night, but brave, beautiful Peony McAllister quickly finished her dinner of Swedish meatballs, Russian tea, English muffins, and Norwegian sardines, put on her fuchsia boots, grabbed her frilly umbrella, and made her lonely way through the inky alley. Terrified, she bumped into a huge, water-soaked box, fell over an abandoned skateboard, and leaped over a muddy puddle. Her nervous laughter echoed through the half-empty garage, but her bright brown eyes found the object of her frantic search, and, as she kick-started her trusty motorcycle, she gave a loud cheer, glad that she wouldn't be late for her nightly Japanese flower-arranging class.

Indefinite Articles (page 7)

1. a unicorn
2. a ham and jam
3. an anchovy
4. A sheriff, a bailiff, a mastiff, an airplane
5. A pirate, an eyepatch
6. An alarming
7. a B, an A

8. a fried-chicken, an abrupt
9. an elephant, an eland, a zebra, an eight-toed
10. an owl's, a bee's
11. a loaf, a half-day
12. an aisle, a grocery, an active
13. a smile, an awful
14. An elm, a locust
15. an ice-cream, an hour

Adverbs (page 9)

Peony McAllister was so excited about her extremely interesting Japanese flower-arranging class that she completely ignored the bright red stop signs randomly placed here and there on her route to school. Suddenly her very cold ears picked up the hauntingly familiar sound of a skull-shatteringly loud siren, and she saw dazzling lights in her rearview mirror. Frantically she began to create convincingly pathetic excuses for going too fast. As she slowly pulled over to the side of the road, she patted her motorcycle tenderly and smiled bravely at the very large person who was slowly approaching.

Conjunctions (page 11)

1. and
2. but
3. so
4. nor
5. yet
6. and, and, and
7. and, or, and

Parts of Speech Exercise 1 (page 12)

"Yes, I tried to pull the wool over your lovely eyes,"
Tom said sheepishly, "and I am very, very sorry."

Common nouns: wool, eyes
Proper nouns: Tom
Pronouns: I, your, I
Verbs: tried, to pull, said, am
Adjectives: the, lovely, sorry
Adverbs: sheepishly, very, very
Prepositions: over
Conjunctions: and
Exclamations: yes

Parts of Speech Exercise 2 (page 13)

The itsy-bitsy, teeny-weeny, yellow polka-dot linguini upset my poor stomach terribly, so I quickly drank some bright pink Pepto-Bismol under the table.

Common nouns: linguini, stomach, table

Proper nouns: Pepto-Bismol

Pronouns: my, I

Verbs: upset, drank

Adjectives: the, itsy-bitsy, teeny-weeny, yellow, polka-dot, poor, pink, the

Adverbs: terribly, quickly, bright

Prepositions: under

Conjunctions: so

Exclamations: —

Parts of Speech Exercise 4 (page 14)

Common nouns:

It was a dark and stormy (night) but brave, beautiful Peony McAllister quickly finished her (dinner) of Swedish (meatballs) Russian (tea) English (muffins) and Norwegian (sardines) put on her fuchsia (boots) grabbed her frilly (umbrella) and made her lonely (way) through the inky (alley) Terrified, she bumped into a huge, water-soaked (box) fell over an abandoned (skateboard) and leaped over a muddy (puddle.) Her nervous (laughter) echoed through the half-empty (garage) but her bright brown (eyes) finally found the (object) of her frantic (search) and, as she kick-started her trusty (motorcycle) she gave a loud (cheer) glad that she wouldn't be late for her nightly Japanese flower-arranging (class.)

Parts of Speech Exercise 5 (page 14)

Adjectives:

Peony McAllister was so (excited) about her extremely (interesting) (Japanese) (flower-arranging) class that she completely ignored the bright (red) stop signs randomly placed here and there on her route to school. Suddenly, her very (cold) ears picked up the hauntingly (familiar) sound of a skull-shatteringly (loud) siren, and she saw (dazzling) lights in her (rearview) mirror. Frantically, she began to create convincingly (pathetic) excuses for going too fast. As she slowly pulled over to the side of the road, she patted her motorcycle tenderly and smiled bravely at the very (large) person who was slowly approaching.

SECTION 2: SENTENCES AND DEPENDENT CLAUSES

Sentence Recognition Exercise 1 (page 21)

1. B	6. C	11. A
2. B	7. A	12. B
3. A	8. C	13. D
4. B	9. A	14. A
5. D	10. C	15. B

Sentence Recognition Exercise 2 (page 24)

7. Who is standing on the desk?
14. You are my favorite person.

SECTION 3: PUNCTUATION

Punctuation Recognition Exercise (page 31)

1. Comma ,
2. Period .
3. Apostrophe '
4. Colon :
5. Semicolon ;
6. Quotation marks " "
7. Question mark ?
8. Exclamation mark !
9. Dash —
10. Parentheses ( )
11. Hyphen -

More Punctuation Recognition

1. Question mark
2. Comma
3. Exclamation mark
4. Quotation marks
5. Semicolon
6. Colon
7. Parentheses
8. Apostrophe
9. Dash
10. Hyphen
11. Period

Comma Rule 1 Exercise (page 32)

1. Let's clap for the Wolf man (, for) he's going to play our song.
2. Chively built a concrete canoe (, but) it wouldn't float.
3. Rambo (and) Rambette like to sit around (and) growl at each other.
4. Mario will win the race (, or) I'll eat my spare tire.

5. My peculiar parakeet doesn't like newspapers, (nor) is he crazy about magazines.

6. You lost the bet, (so) you have to march behind the elephants in the parade.

7. You're trying to gain weight, (yet) you're still eating birdseed salad.

8. George (and) Martha invited Jim (and) Dolly over for ice cream (and) cake, (but) Dolly fell (and) skinned her knee, (so) they couldn't go.

9. We went camping last week, (but) we forgot the cooler (and) the tent, (so) we came home early.

10. You did all the digging, (so) the treasure is yours.

Comma Rule 2 Exercise (page 34)

1. nails, tacks, and staples
2. no commas
3. no commas
4. coughs, sputters, and stalls
5. no commas
6. coffee, tea, or chokecherry juice
7. Halloween, Labor Day, and Martin Van Buren's Birthday.
8. Dopey, Doc, Sneezy, and Grumpy.
9. Bashful, Sleepy, and Happy
10. Larry, Curly, and Mo instead of Groucho, Harpo, and Zeppo

Comma Rule 3 Exercise (page 36)

1. As soon as the bank opens,
2. OK
3. When I found a rattlesnake in the dryer,
4. OK
5. OK
6. If you park on the sidewalk,
7. OK
8. Because you're my friend,
9. When you go to the store,
10. OK

Punctuation Exercise (page 36)

1. no commas
2. no commas
3. red hair, green eyes, and orange noses

4. I cleaned Mongo's room, and then I locked the door, so

5. You take the high road, and I'll take the bus.

6. Cosmic Clashes concert, but they said

7. his wallet, his car keys, and his lucky rabbit's foot

8. the hook, line, and sinker and then started on the lock, stock, and barrel

9. at the fair, but our wombat

10. The bus is leaving, so run for it!

11. no commas

12. When I'm sixty-four,

13. Mrs. Bridges, Mr. Udson, and Rose

14. If I wear a purple potato sack to the party,

15. no commas

16. Although you are my favorite person,

17. vinegar, but what

18. Matt is a standup comic, so he doesn't own any chairs.

19. in the woodwork, but it's still my home, and I love it

20. with the circus, but she was tired

21. puce, chartreuse, and aubergine, but I think

22. If you'll put your trombone away,

23. growl and snarl, so they

24. the paving machine, so she calls him Leotarred

25. Get down, jump back, and cool out.

Comma Rule 4 Exercise (page 38)

1. The tall, awkward stranger stepped on my tired, aching foot.

2. The <u>friendly</u> tiger rolled over and revealed his
   ④
   <u>fuzzy, fat</u> tummy.
3. The bright <u>purple</u> skateboard took off on its
   ④
   own down the <u>steep, winding</u> hill.
   ④
4. <u>Stately, plump</u> Buck Mulligan made <u>some</u>
   ④
   <u>hot, delicious</u> stew.
   ④
5. The <u>short, chubby</u> porcupine got stuck under
   ④
   the <u>dirty, dented</u> truck.
   ④
6. The <u>handsome</u> actor swung on the <u>long,</u>
   <u>tangled</u> vines and landed on a crocodile.
   ④
7. The <u>hostile, sleepy</u> neighbors complained
   ④
   about your <u>wild, noisy</u> party.
   ④ (optional)
8. The <u>popular, young</u> rock star tripped over his
   ④
   <u>long, curly</u> microphone cord.
9. The very <u>sweet little</u> chimpanzee gave me a
   ④
   <u>sticky, sour</u> lollipop.
10. The <u>six enormous old pink</u> elephants pranced
    through my very <u>troubled</u> dreams.

Comma Rule 5 Exercise (page 38)

1. We're running out of ice, naturally, because of
   ⑤   ⑤
   the heat wave.
2. I plan, come heck or high water, to see that
   ⑤   ⑤
   new movie tonight.
3. Aphasia and Inertia, however, have already
   ⑤   ⑤
   seen it twice.
4. They told me, despite my protests, the whole
   ⑤   ⑤
   story.
5. I will, therefore, hide the last chapter of the
   ⑤   ⑤
   suspense novel they're reading.
6. Mongo is, according to his mother, Mr.
   ⑤   ⑤
   Congeniality.
7. He lost his temper, though, last week.
   ⑤   ⑤
8. He flew into a ring-tailed snit, by golly.
   ⑤

Comma Rule 6 Exercise (page 39)

1. Stuck in the hula hoop, Mr. Jellyby
   ⑥
   whimpered.
2. Rising to the surface, the diver wiped mud
   ⑥
   from her eyes.
3. Stranded at the mall, Clorene and Florene
   ⑥
   shopped till they dropped.
4. Worried about shortages at the post office,
   ⑥
   Rambo and Rambette started a stampede.
5. Dazzled by my rhinestone earrings, the
   ⑥
   burglar bumped into a chair.
6. no comma
7. no comma
8. Her eyes sparkling, Lizzo sharpened her wits.
   ⑥
9. Stunned by the thunder, the possum played
   ⑥
   dead.
10. Forgotten by his fans, the former football
    ⑥
    hero wept.
11. Laughing and singing, the Bobbsey twins
    ⑥
    repaired the tricycle.
12. Living in the Midwest, I see a lot of
    ⑥
    spectacular sunsets.
13. Flattened by the boulder, the flower wilted
    ⑥
    and died.
14. Defeated by the Roadrunner, the coyote
    ⑥
    gnashed his teeth.
15. Missing his target, the hunter decided to
    ⑥
    clean his glasses.

Comma Rule 7 Exercise (page 41)

1. Mr. Legree, the owner of the apartment
   ⑦
   building, loves ferns and petunias.
   ⑦
2. The town philosopher, Soda Crates McGurk,
   ⑦   ⑦
   sits on a cracker barrel.
3. OK
4. My grandmother, an engineer, plays bridge
   ⑦   ⑦
   every working day.

5. Monstro Suggins, who has 196 pigs, collects silk purses.⁷⁷

6. OK

7. OK

8. This is my house, which needs to be painted.⁷

9. Uncle Elmo, the game warden, hates poached eggs.⁷⁷

10. OK

11. OK

12. I ordered my favorite snack, which is⁷

    albatross-on-a-stick and chokecherry juice, at the Miss Tucson diner.⁷

13. OK

14. OK

15. We sent a card to Chively Sneed, who's in the hospital because he's allergic to chicken.⁷

16. Jason, the leader of the neighborhood kazoo⁷

    band, is tone-deaf.⁷

17. We finally talked to Mr. Ed, who was a little hoarse.⁷

18. My mother, who was Mrs. America in 1925, still has a radiant smile.⁷⁷

19. Rambette, whose sister wears combat boots, is my best friend.⁷⁷

20. OK

Comma Rule 8 Exercise (page 42)

1. We are here, my friends, to mourn the passing of my pet python.⁸⁸

2. Please eat your birdseed, Tweetie.⁸

3. Mongo, I have barricaded your room.⁸

4. Ladies and gentlemen, may I have your attention?⁸

5. Today, boys and girls, we're going to search for elves.⁸⁸

6. no commas

7. Are you ready for a new star, Hollywood?⁸

8. no commas

9. Fedonia Krump, come here this instant!⁸

10. My fellow Americans, my rubber ducky has sprung a leak.⁸

Comma Rule 9 Exercise (page 43)

1. No, I'd rather not go to aerobics class in snowshoes.⁹

2. Well, let me say this about that.⁹

3. Nevertheless, you promised you'd make marshmallow soup today.⁹

4. Finally, Rambo and Rambette got their new bazooka.⁹

5. Yes, I'll help you housebreak your new wombat.⁹

6. At long last, we can go to the flea festival.⁹

7. Therefore, we won't be here for your demolition derby.⁹

8. After all, there's no place like home.⁹

9. Oh, please don't fence me in.⁹

10. In conclusion, I'd like to invite you to tour the salt mine.⁹

Comma Rule 10 Exercise (page 44)

1. The cave is dark, and it's smelly, too.¹⁰

2. We, too, must march with flaming torches to the castle.¹⁰¹⁰

3. If Rambette gets a new grenade, I deserve one, too.¹⁰

4. If you get up early, be sure to go to bed early, too.¹⁰

5. No comma needed—*too* doesn't mean *also* here

6. No comma needed—*too* doesn't mean *also* here

7. Are your children night owls, too?¹⁰

8. This water balloon is too small, and it's leaky, ⑩
too.

9. If you're too nervous to explore the haunted
house, I'll stay home, too. ⑩

10. Cinderella scrubbed the dungeon and drained
the moat, too. ⑩

11. Are you, too, turning down the Caesar salad, ⑩ ⑩
Brutus?

12. Too, we must do our homework before we go ⑩
to sleep.

13. We, too, would like some purple cotton candy ⑩ ⑩
at the fair.

14. Grandpa loves to waltz, and Grandma does, ⑩
too.

15. Geraniums are pretty, and they smell nice, ⑩
too.

Comma Rule 11 Exercise (page 44)

1. You're not afraid of the eight-toed wombat, ⑪
are you?

2. Aphasia won the watermelon-juggling contest, ⑪
didn't she?

3. I washed the parakeet last night, didn't I? ⑪

4. Good fences make good neighbors, don't ⑪
they?

5. The television set overheated and exploded
during your favorite program, didn't it? ⑪

6. No comma is needed—this is a real question.

7. You know the way to Buzzards Bay, don't ⑪
you?

8. No comma is needed—this is a real question.

9. Spring was a little late this year, wasn't it? ⑪

10. The boss wants us to go home early, doesn't ⑪
she?

Comma Rule 12 Exercise (page 45)

1. To begin with, diamonds are expensive. ⑫

2. To you, toads are adorable. ⑫

3. To Peggy, Sue was very polite. ⑫

4. In 1988, 999 wombats mysteriously ⑫
disappeared.

5. In the water, lilies are a lovely sight. ⑫

6. Whenever possible, pit bulls are to be avoided. ⑫

7. In this school, teachers are often asked for ⑫
their autographs.

8. As a matter of fact, finding Mongo's house is ⑫
tricky.

9. Walking, the dog got as far as the corner. ⑫

10. To you, perfect people are boring. ⑫

Semicolon Rule 13 Exercise (pages 46–47)

1. It rained last night; there are puddles ⑬
everywhere today.

2. It rained last night, so there are puddles ①
everywhere today.

3. The teacher was nervous, and he dropped the ①
chalk ten times.

4. The teacher was nervous; he dropped the ⑬
chalk ten times.

5. No punctuation is needed.

6. No punctuation is needed.

7. You're brave and polite; I admire you. ⑬

8. You're brave and polite, so I admire you. ①

9. Peony and Chively cooked and cleaned; Mongo ⑬
and Fedonia whined and complained.

10. Tuesday is payday, so let's celebrate. ①

Exercise in Semicolon Rule 13 and Commas with Conjunctive Adverbs (page 48)

1. Those fuchsia boots are inexpensive; in fact, ⑬
they cost less than a new shirt.

2. Those fuchsia boots are inexpensive; they ⑬
cost less, in fact, than a new shirt.

3. Those fuchsia boots are inexpensive; they cost less than a new shirt, in fact. ⑬

4. I'm too tired to go skydiving; moreover, my parachute is torn. ⑬

5. I'm too tired to go skydiving; my parachute is torn, moreover. ⑬

6. I'm too tired to go skydiving; my parachute, moreover, is torn. ⑬

7. No punctuation is needed.

8. No punctuation is needed.

9. I am a Taurus; therefore, you can't change my mind. ⑬

10. I am a Taurus; you can't, therefore, change my mind. ⑬

or

Semicolon Rule 14 Exercise (page 49)

1. Fedonia adopted a new wombat in November, 1930; August, 1949; and April, 1973. ⑭ ⑭

2. Rambo and Rambette have destroyed sections of Caribou, Maine; Troy, New York; and Northampton, Massachusetts. ⑭ ⑭

3. Grandma Pringle has lived at 4092 Silver Street, Carson City, Nevada; 681 Dolphin Drive, Miami, Florida; 2903 Rook Road, Atlantic City, New Jersey; and 666 Beefcake Boulevard, Los Angeles, California. ⑭ ⑭ ⑭

4. Aphasia wore mittens, earmuffs, and long underwear to the tiddlywinks tournament. ② ②

5. Gloria Muldoon, a radiologist; Alvin Krebs, a banker; Joan Rio, a juggler; and Barbara Doucette, a welder, received awards at the banquet. ⑭ ⑭ ⑭

Colon Rule 15 Exercise (page 50)

1. Please deliver the following at noon tomorrow: five tons of gravel, a gallon of insect repellent, an ant farm, and nine caterpillars. ⑮

2. Our house has all the modern conveniences: electricity, indoor plumbing, screen doors, and a lightning rod. ⑮

3. Junior slyly hid the following under his sister's bed: snakes, snails, a rat's skeleton, barbed wire, and a live skunk. ⑮

4. Our swim team is planning to offer lessons in all the popular strokes: the Australian crawl, the backstroke, the breast stroke, and the dog paddle. ⑮

Fun and Games with Punctuation (page 53)

When the very large person reached Peony, ③ who was pulled over to the side of the road, her stom- ⑦ ⑦ ach started to ache, and she regretted her speedy din- ① ner of Swedish meatballs, Russian tea, English ② ② muffins, and Norwegian sardines. "Good evening, of- ② ⑧ ficer," she said cheerfully, but she was, in fact, in tur- ① ⑤ ⑤ moil. The very large person slowly removed his ① You could use Rule 5 commas instead of sunglasses, and Peony started wondering why (on parentheses here such a dark and stormy night) sunglasses were ① needed at all, but she decided not to ask. ① Meanwhile, the lights on the vehicle that had parked ⑨ behind her motorcycle continued to flash, and the ① siren kept screaming, too. "That's a lovely sequin ⑩ headband you have there, sir," Peony said in her very ⑧ nicest tone. The very large person grunted, "Yo." Peony admitted that she might have been going just a bit too fast. "Yo," the very large person grunted again. "You see, it's almost midnight, and the daylilies ⑨ or ⑫ ① will expire before I can arrange them artistically for the final exam in my Japanese flower-arranging class." "Yo," the very large person grunted yet again. "Wait a minute!" cried Peony. "Didn't I see an article about you in last week's issue of *Film Flam*, the movie ⑦ magazine?" Blushing, the very large person looked ⑫

⑨
shyly at the ground. "Aw, shucks," he said. "I was just playing with my new flashing lights and skull-shat-

①
teringly loud siren, and I guess I got carried away. You

⑪   ⑤
won't tell anybody you saw me, will you?" Peony, of

⑤
course, replied that she would carry his secret to her

⑬   ⑦
grave; however, she did ask for his autograph, which he etched with his dagger into the handlebar of her

⑫ or ⑤ or parentheses ⑫   ⑭
motorcycle. "This, along with June 6, 1960; February

⑭   ⑫   ⑫ or ⑤ or parentheses
21, 1962; and January 20, 1964, is one of my favorite days of all time," said Peony. The very large person

①
(who shall remain nameless, but we all know who he

⑪   ④
is, don't we?) then returned to his flashing, screaming vehicle and sped off into the night. Peony gazed lovingly at the autograph that honored her handlebar

②   ②
and then slowly, carefully, and joyfully continued on her way to the flower-arranging final exam where she overwhelmed the teacher by gluing a daylily to her motorcycle and attaching a poem entitled "Putting the Petal to the Metal."

Last Exercise in Rules 1, 2, 3, and 13 Before the Test (page 53)

①
1. Chively hates fried chicken, so Fedonia never serves it.

③
2. Because Chively hates fried chicken, Fedonia never serves it.

⑬
3. Chively hates fried chicken; therefore, Fedonia never serves it.

⑬
4. Chively hates fried chicken; Fedonia never serves it.

5. No punctuation is needed

②
6. Peony has studied flower arranging, igloo
②
building, and fudge making.

②   ②
7. Peony plans to visit Japan, Alaska, and Mackinac Island.

8. No punctuation is needed

③
9. Because Peony enjoys studying and traveling, she's very interesting.

10. No punctuation is needed.

①
11. Peony enjoys studying and traveling, so she is very interesting.

⑬
12. Peony enjoys studying and traveling; she is very interesting.

⑬
13. Peony enjoys studying and traveling; therefore, she is very interesting.

⑬
14. Peony enjoys studying and traveling; she is, therefore, very interesting.

⑬
15. Peony enjoys studying and traveling; she is very interesting, therefore.

⑬
16. Peony is practically perfect in every way; she makes me want to scream.

17. I wish Peony would take a long walk on a
⑬
short pier; I'm not very nice.

②   ②   ②
18. Inertia, Aphasia, and Mongo thrive on clutter,
②
turmoil, and anxiety.

②   ②
19. Although Inertia, Aphasia, and Mongo thrive
②   ②   ③
on clutter, turmoil, and anxiety, they manage to get their work done on time.

②   ②   ②
20. Inertia, Aphasia, and Mongo thrive on clutter,
②   ⑬
turmoil, and anxiety; however, they manage to get their work done on time.

②   ②   ②
21. Inertia, Aphasia, and Mongo thrive on clutter,
②   ⑬
turmoil, and anxiety; they manage, however, to get their work done on time.

②   ②   ②
22. Inertia, Aphasia, and Mongo thrive on clutter,
②   ①
turmoil, and anxiety, but they manage to get their work done on time.

23. When we have finished this exercise, we can take a break.

24. No punctuation is needed.

①
25. We have finished this exercise, so let's take a break.

SECTION 4: SENTENCE VARIETY, SENTENCE-COMBINING, AND SENTENCE-WRITING

Sentence Variety and Sentence-Combining Exercise (page 58)

There are several possibilities for each sentence; the shortest versions appear here, just for guidance.

1. Our dog howls all night, and our cat snarls all day, so our neighbors are moving.
2. When the speeding car got a flat tire, it went off the road.
3. I got sick at the fair yesterday because I went on the Ferris wheel after I ate cotton candy, soft pretzels, and candied apples and drank four cups of lemonade.
4. Nobody got any work done when my boss had an all-morning meeting last week.
5. Elmo removed the drainpipe after his wombat got caught in it twice.
6. The goldfish is very thin because it eats only dandelion seeds, which are scarce in the winter.
7. I plan to make squid stew for dinner, but there is no squid in the house, so I'll have to go to the store to get some.
8. This morning, the big, fat, mean canary from next door bent the bars on its cage, flew into my kitchen, and tore my apron to shreds while I was making toast. (WHEW!)

SECTION 5: SINGULARS, PLURALS, POSSESSIVES, AND CONTRACTIONS

Exercise in Singulars and Plurals (page 64)

1. P lady
2. P rainbow
3. S men
4. P bird
5. P loaf
6. S brushes
7. S children
8. P woman
9. P loss
10. S women
11. P ox
12. P glass
13. S ladies
14. P toy
15. P waitress
16. S and P
17. P child
18. P emergency
19. P buzz
20. P church
21. P witch
22. S and P
23. S media
24. P tooth

25. P crisis
26. P baboon
27. P monkey
28. P turkey
29. S geese
30. S phenomena

Singular Possessives Exercise (page 65)

1. woman's
2. ox's
3. desk's
4. boss's
5. mirror's
6. child's
7. goose's
8. country's
9. pen's
10. glass's

Plural Possessives Exercise (page 66)

singular	plural	ending	add	plural possessive form
analysis	analyses	s	'	analyses'
woman	women	not s	's	women's
child	children	not s	's	children's
mother	mothers	s	'	mothers'
box	boxes	s	'	boxes'
dress	dresses	s	'	dresses'
monkey	monkeys	s	'	monkeys'
salary	salaries	s	'	salaries'
foot	feet	not s	's	feet's
sheep	sheep	not s	's	sheep's
mouse	mice	not s	's	mice's
house	houses	s	'	houses'
pencil	pencils	s	'	pencils'
book	books	s	'	books'
cry	cries	s	'	cries'

Contractions Exercise 1 (page 68)

1. don't
2. I'm
3. you've
4. he's
5. we're
6. they're
7. doesn't
8. they could've danced
9. she might've seen
10. I should've gone
11. it'll
12. who's
13. who's
14. it's
15. it's
16. he can't
17. the taxi's
18. she won't
19. she wouldn't
20. Fedonia's
21. it didn't
22. I shouldn't
23. they couldn't
24. he hasn't

Contractions Exercise 2 (page 68)

1.	cannot	13.	were not
2.	have not	14.	does not
3.	you are	15.	who is *or* who has
4.	he is	16.	did not
5.	we are	17.	that is
6.	we will	18.	Rambo is
7.	they have	19.	the teacher is
8.	they are	20.	he would
9.	do not	21.	they could have gone
10.	it is *or* it has	22.	I might have died
11.	you have been	23.	she should have seen
12.	it will	24.	who has been sleeping

How to Tell the Difference Between Possessives and Contractions Exercise (page 69)

1.	C	Cinderella	9.	C	wombat
2.	P	knees	10.	C	Mongo
3.	C	boy	11.	P	suitcase
4.	P	loneliness	12.	C	Mongo
5.	P	crown	13.	C	Mongo
6.	C	queen	14.	C	play
7.	P	fur	15.	P	author
8.	P	feet			

The Third Use of the Apostrophe Exercise (page 70)

1.	4's	6.	antidisestablishmentarianism's
2.	73's	7.	s's
3.	='s	8.	q's
4.	*'s	9.	fantastic's
5.	#'s	10.	%'s

SECTION 6: PRONOUNS, TRICKY WORDS THAT SOUND ALIKE, DOUBLE NEGATIVES, AND NEEDLESS REPETITION

Subject Pronouns Exercise (page 78)

1.	she	3.	it	5.	they
2.	they	4.	he		

Objects Pronouns Exercise (page 79)

1.	her	2.	him	3.	them

Exercise in Subject and Object Personal Pronouns (page 79)

1.	O	10.	S	18.	S
2.	S	11.	O	19.	S
3.	O	12.	S	20.	O
4.	O	13.	O	21.	S
5.	S	14.	O	22.	S
6.	O	15.	S	23.	O
7.	S	16.	S	24.	O
8.	O	17.	O	25.	S
9.	S				

Another Place for the Subject Pronoun Exercise (page 81)

1.	she	3.	we	5.	they
2.	he	4.	I		

Pronoun Exercise (page 83)

1.	We	12.	me
2.	her	13.	I
3.	I	14.	We
4.	him and me	15.	she, us
5.	me	16.	We
6.	He and she	17.	she
7.	me	18.	her
8.	We	19.	him and her
9.	him and me	20.	He, she, we, and they
10.	He and I		him, her, us, and them
11.	she		

Possessive Personal Pronouns Exercise (page 84)

1.	your	6.	Their, yours
2.	Their	7.	theirs
3.	yours	8.	ours
4.	their	9.	It's
5.	hers	10.	its

Another Tricky Pronoun Exercise (page 85)

1. whom	6. whom
2. Who	7. whom
3. Who's	8. Who's
4. Whose	9. Who
5. Whoever	10. Who's, who

Exercise in Pronoun Agreement (page 88)

1. his	3. his	5. their
2. it makes	4. her	

Exercise in Reflexive Pronouns (page 89)

1. me	6. herself
2. I	7. himself
3. me	8. themselves
4. myself	9. me
5. yourself	10. himself

Tricky Words Exercise (page 91)

1. You're, your
2. its, its, its
3. You're, your, too
4. Who's, they're
5. There is too much sin in Cincinnati.
6. It's after midnight, so I guess they're not coming.
7. Whose house is being used for the party, and who's going to be there?
8. It's too bad that your canary chased their cat up a tree.
9. Their landlord lowered their rent, so they're very happy; they've lived there for eight years.
10. It's snowing too hard for your wombat to find its way home.
11. I'd like to go to Graceland, too, but it's too far to ask your mother to drive us.
12. Whose Winnebago is blocking the driveway, and who's going to volunteer to move it?
13. It's not too great an idea to let Mongo eat too much cotton candy before he rides the Frightmobile.
14. It's been too tempting to look at the last page of the detective story, but I won't ruin your fun by telling you whose body was found in the chandelier.

15. The wombats wanted to learn to dance, too, but the samba was too fast for their stubby little legs.

Exercise in Double Negatives (page 94)

1. I haven't ever seen a purple cow.
   I have never seen a purple cow.
2. There isn't any cranberry juice in the refrigerator.
   There is no cranberry juice in the refrigerator.
3. OK
4. OK (there's only one negative in each clause, and that's legal)
5. OK
6. Grandma Pringle can hardly twirl her baton.
   Grandma Pringle can't twirl her baton.
7. My mother hasn't ever been to Australia.
   My mother has never been to Australia.
8. I can't help loving my dog.
9. OK (let's hear you sing it!)
10. OK
11. My birthday isn't anything special, so don't go to any trouble.
    My birthday is nothing special, so go to no trouble.
    My birthday is nothing special, so don't go to any trouble.
    My birthday isn't anything special, so go to no trouble.
12. I couldn't help weeping when there wasn't any surprise party.
    I couldn't help weeping when there was no surprise party.
13. They dug up the beach, but they didn't find any treasure.
    They dug up the beach, but they found no treasure.
14. OK
15. Mongo's not going anywhere.
    Mongo is going nowhere.
16. I can hardly look at another garbanzo bean.
    I can't look at another garbanzo bean.
17. Senator Mudhen can't help getting into trouble.
18. OK
19. Lizzo is scarcely old enough to drive, but she owns a bulldozer.
    Lizzo isn't old enough to drive, but she owns a bulldozer.

20. You aren't going anywhere with that flat tire.
You are going nowhere with that flat tire.

Needless Repetition Exercise (page 96)

1. The snake's hissing was barely audible.
2. The mustard stain on my shirt is scarcely visible.
3. The glass bowl magnifies the fish.
The glass bowl makes the fish look bigger.
4. Then, I was in seventh grade.
5. You're really making terrific progress.
Really, you're making terrific progress.
6. When you open an account at Ferguson Federal, you'll get a gift.
7. Leave out any unnecessary marshmallows.
Omit any unnecessary marshmallows.
Leave out any marshmallows you don't need.
Omit any marshmallows you don't need.
8. Combine anchovies and peanut butter for an unusual salad.
9. This is the last announcement of our sale on wombat houses.
This is the final announcement of our sale on wombat houses.
10. Please repeat the address.
Please say the address again.
11. Mongo reports for duty at 8 P.M.
Mongo reports for duty at eight o'clock at night.
12. Please meet me under the clock at McDonald's at noon.
13. Fedonia's stuffed animals dance and sing at midnight.
14. In my opinion, leather earrings are nifty.
I think leather earrings are nifty.
15. *The Broom of the System* is a bestseller.

SECTION 7: VERBS

Exercise in Subject-Verb Agreement (page 103)

1. <u>members</u> have
2. <u>hands</u> make
3. <u>apple</u> Does
4. <u>dogs and English-men</u> go
5. <u>grin</u> is
6. <u>cooks</u> are
7. I like
8. <u>pineapple or mango</u> makes
9. <u>pineapple and mango</u> are
10. <u>bells</u> are <u>they</u> haven't

11. <u>Mongo</u> has <u>he</u> doesn't
12. <u>One</u> has <u>she</u> eats
13. <u>bug</u> is <u>kinds</u> are
14. <u>rain</u> falls
15. <u>Issues</u> have
16. <u>Neither</u> wears
17. <u>Both</u> like
18. <u>smoke</u> is <u>you</u> are
19. <u>One</u> is
20. <u>recipe and mixer</u> are

Tense Exercise (page 112)

1. future
2. future
3. present
4. simple past
5. present
6. simple past
7. future
8. present
9. simple past
10. present
11. future
12. present
13. future
14. simple past
15. simple past

Conjugation Exercise (page 113)

to miss *in the present tense:*
I **miss,** you **miss,** he, she, or it **misses**
we **miss,** you **miss,** they **miss**

to bathe *in the simple past tense:*
I **bathed,** you **bathed,** he, she, or it **bathed**
we **bathed,** you **bathed,** they **bathed**

to smile *in the future tense:*
I **will smile,** you **will smile,** he, she, or it **will smile**
we **will smile,** you **will smile,** they **will smile**

Another Verb Exercise (page 114)

to zork

5. in the present tense: I **zork,** you **zork,** he, she, or it **zorks,** we **zork,** you **zork,** they **zork**
6. in the simple past tense: I **zorked,** you **zorked,** he, she, or it **zorked,** we **zorked,** you **zorked,** they **zorked**
7. in the future tense: I **will zork,** you **will zork,** he, she, or it **will zork,** we **will zork,** you **will zork,** they **will zork**

Conjugation Exercise (page 115)

to smile *in the present perfect tense:*
I **have smiled,** you **have smiled,** he, she, or it **has smiled**
we **have smiled,** you **have smiled,** they **have smiled**

Past Perfect Exercise (page 116)

The sentence should include **had smiled.**

Future Perfect Exercise (page 116)

The sentence should include **will have smiled.**

Another Small Exercise (page 116)

> *to fiffle* in the present perfect tense:
> I **have fiffled,** you **have fiffled,** he, she, or it **has fiffled**
> we **have fiffled,** you **have fiffled,** they **have fiffled**

> *to fiffle* in the past perfect tense:
> I **had fiffled,** you **had fiffled,** he, she, or it **had fiffled**
> we **had fiffled,** you **had fiffled,** they **had fiffled**

Present Progressive Exercise (page 117)

Here is the conjugation of *to laugh* in the present progressive tense, so the sentence should include one of these forms:

> I **am laughing,** you **are laughing,** he, she, or it **is laughing,** we **are laughing,** you **are laughing,** they **are laughing**

Past Progressive Exercise (page 118)

Here is the conjugation of *to laugh* in the past progressive tense, so the sentence should include one of these forms:

> I **was laughing,** you **were laughing,** he, she, or it **was laughing,** we **were laughing,** you **were laughing,** they **were laughing**

Future Progressive Exercise (page 118)

The sentence should include **will be laughing.**

Present Perfect Progressive Exercise (page 118)

Here is the conjugation of *to laugh* in the present perfect progressive tense, so the sentence should contain one of these forms:

> I **have been laughing,** you **have been laughing,** he, she, or it **has been laughing,** we **have been laughing,** you **have been laughing,** they **have been laughing**

One More Conjugation Exercise (page 119)

> *to greble* in the present progressive tense:
> I **am grebling,** you **are grebling,** he, she, or it **is grebling**
> we **are grebling,** you **are grebling,** they **are grebling**

> *to greble* in the present perfect progressive tense:
> I **have been grebling,** you **have been grebling,** he, she, or it **has been grebling**
> we **have been grebling,** you **have been grebling,** they **have been grebling**

> *to greble* in the future progressive tense:
> I **will be grebling,** you **will be grebling,** he, she, or it **will be grebling**
> we **will be grebling,** you **will be grebling,** they **will be grebling**

More Tense Exercises

A: Present Progressive Exercise (page 119)

1. We **are picking** buttercups behind the barn.
2. She **is singing** sad songs in the moonlight.
3. Jaws, my pet wombat, **is eating** my license plate.
4. Rambette **is tossing** grenades at the termites.
5. Grandma **is buying** a plastic dress.

B: Present Perfect Exercise (page 120)

1. I **have lost** my patience with this wretched computer.
2. **Have** you **gone** to the Cosmic Clashes concert?
3. Many **have volunteered,** but few **have been** reliable.
4. I **have eaten** three packages of cream horns for breakfast.
5. **Have** you **lived** here?

C: Past Perfect Exercise (page 120)

1. Someone **had left** the cake out in the rain.
2. London Bridge **had fallen** down; we can hardly expect it to fall up.
3. You **had used** the last little bit of toothpaste.
4. She **had eaten** only bee brains and ant livers for a whole week.
5. The mean crocodile **had** completely **demolished** Tarzan's waterwings.

D: Past Progressive Exercise (page 120)

1. Mongo **was sweeping** the dust bunnies into the mailbox.
2. I **was looking** for a silver lining in the cloud.
3. Peony **was riding** her motorcycle all over the Southwest.
4. **Were** you **buying** some chokecherry cookies at the bakery?
5. The gerbils **were escaping** through a hole in the ceiling.

Fun With Verbs *(page 120)*

1. OK, did
2. knew, has seen
3. saw, were going
4. OK, burst
5. have brought, brought
6. has done, saw (*or* has seen)
7. might have thought, OK
8. said, has seen, has tried
9. OK, OK
10. has taken, OK, left
11. brought, threw
12. shrank, wept
13. asked, slid, OK
14. sang, sank, OK, stank
15. OK, OK, OK, OK

Exercise in Needless Tense Shifts *(page 122)*

1. OK
2. Whenever the teacher talks to them, their faces squinch up.
3. I saw a tall, dark, handsome pirate in the pond, so I fainted.
4. OK
5. King Kong started to think sweet thoughts, so he stopped eating honey.

Exercise in Recognizing Verbs in the Passive Voice *(page 123)*

1. passive stew
2. active cooks
3. passive house
4. active termites
5. passive he
6. active Red Cross
7. active chandelier
8. passive party
9. passive Rambo
10. active mouse
11. passive concert
12. active Howling Skitters
13. active Mongo
14. passive check
15. passive I
16. active alarm clock
17. passive hiker
18. active Royal Canadian Mounted Police
19. passive Grandpa
20. active aroma

Exercise in Changing Passive Verbs to Active Verbs *(page 125)*

1. Absent-minded Bo Peep lost the sheep.
2. The students' smiles encouraged the teacher.
3. The wind blew my tent away.
4. The circus hired Chuckles the Clown.
5. The princess's kiss changed the frog into a handsome accountant.
6. The tailor made the pants too long.
7. The escaped chimpanzee stole the bananas.
8. Curiosity killed the cat.
9. Cinderella decorated the dungeon.
10. Termites ate the dancer's wooden shoes.

Active–Passive Mixtures Exercise *(page 126)*

1. She received your bill, and she threw it into the well.
2. The witch melted Plastic Man and turned him into a credit card.
3. OK
4. Grandma set the table while Grandpa mashed the turnips.
5. The hungry pirate stole the chickens, and we suspected foul play.

Transitive and Intransitive Verbs Exercise *(page 128)*

1. i
2. t critter
3. i
4. t critter sandwich
5. i
6. t Larry's hand
7. i
8. t vow
9. t critter sandwich
10. i

To sit/To set Exercise *(page 130)*

1. sits
2. sat
3. set
4. Set
5. sat

To lie/To lay Exercise (page 130)

1.	lies	3.	lay	5.	lain
2.	lay	4.	Lay		

To rise/To raise Exercise (page 131)

1.	raised	3.	raised	5.	rose
2.	will rise	4.	rose		

Exercise in Confusing Verbs (page 131)

1.	sitting	6.	lay	11.	lain
2.	raise	7.	rise	12.	laid
3.	raise	8.	rose	13.	raised
4.	rise	9.	lie	14.	laid
5.	laid	10.	laid	15.	set

Exercise in Linking Verbs (page 134)

1. L   terrible
2. L   bitter
3. L   comfortable
4. L   good
5. L   hungry   thirsty   sore
6. L   bad
7. L   odd
8. L   good
9. A   cautiously
10. A   slowly
11. L   notorious
12. L   weird

SECTION 8: BITS OF FASCINATION

Participle Exercise (page 140)

1.	noun	6.	noun
2.	adjective	7.	adjective
3.	verb	8.	verb
4.	verb	9.	verb
5.	adjective	10.	adjective

Gerund Exercise (page 141)

1. **Your** falling asleep in the middle of my speech hurt my feelings.
2. **His** driving at 175 miles per hour through town makes me nervous.

3. **Mongo's** teasing his sister got him into a lot of trouble yesterday.
4. The **canary's** chasing cats is not a good thing to do.
5. **Their** tying the babysitter to a tree is the last straw.

Exercise in Recognizing Dangling Participles (page 142)

1.	dang	tide	11.	dang	child
2.	OK	message	12.	OK	monsters
3.	dang	I	13.	OK	sheets
4.	OK	spoon	14.	dang	I
5.	dang	cane	15.	OK	car
6.	OK	grandmother	16.	dang	mechanic
7.	OK	bomb	17.	dang	boat
8.	dang	boss	18.	OK	sailor
9.	dang	we	19.	dang	shoelace
10.	OK	frog	20.	OK	I

Misplaced Modifiers Exercise (page 145)

1. The ambulance drivers took the accident **victim** with the broken leg to the hospital.
2. The **clown** with the red rubber nose kissed the woman.
3. **Steak** that was swimming in gravy was served by the chef.
   The chef served steak that was swimming in gravy.
4. OK
5. The nurse's **uniform** that was stiff with starch hung in the closet.

Two-Way Adverb Exercise (page 146)

1. People who truly love music dance well.
   People who love music dance truly well.
2. Anyone who frequently watches television sees commercials.
   Anyone who watches television sees commercials frequently.
3. Adults who often whine are lonely.
   Adults who whine are lonely often.
4. People who seldom exercise have back trouble.
   People who exercise have back trouble seldom.

5. Students who daily forget their books are in trouble.
Students who forget their books are in trouble daily.

Parallelism Exercise (page 146)

1. Ma praised Mongo for being thoughtful and prompt.
Ma praised Mongo for thoughtfulness and promptness.
2. Skeeter McClure is small, quick, and athletic.
Skeeter McClure is a small, quick athlete.
3. He promised to clean his room and to take out the trash.
He promised that he would clean his room and take out the trash.
4. Riding the bus is less expensive than driving a car.
To ride the bus is less expensive than to drive a car.
5. The old house needs new wiring, new insulation, and a new coat of paint.
The old house needs to be given new wiring, new insulation, and a new coat of paint.

Exercise in Degrees of Adjectives and Adverbs (page 149)

Positive	Comparative	Superlative
cheerful	more cheerful	most cheerful
much	more	most
wonderful	more wonderful	most wonderful
cautiously	more cautiously	most cautiously
nice	nicer	nicest
eager	more eager	most eager
good	better	best
splendid	more splendid	most splendid
many	more	most
quietly	more quietly	most quietly
shyly	more shyly	most shyly
generous	more generous	most generous
well	better	best
apathetic	more apathetic	most apathetic
flexible	more flexible	most flexible
fascinating	more fascinating	most fascinating
hypnotically	more hypnotically	most hypnotically
enormous	more enormous	most enormous
ambitious	more ambitious	most ambitious
lackadaisically	more lackadaisically	most lackadaisically
rude	ruder	rudest
unsuccessful	more unsuccessful	most unsuccessful
courageous	more courageous	most courageous
bad	worse	worst
late	later	latest

Exercise in Using Words Correctly (page 155)

1. etc.
2. a
3. aggravated
4. irritated
5. between
6. among
7. everyday
8. every day
9. broke
10. then
11. nauseated
12. than
13. parachute
14. Regardless
15. further
16. fewer
17. for
18. supposed
19. that
20. from
21. as
22. her
23. fewer
24. a lot
25. used
26. farther

SECTION 9: PARAGRAPHS

Exercise in Recognizing Topic Sentences (page 164)

A.
8. I don't like to write personal letters.

B.
4. My nose is the one thing I would change about myself if I could.

Exercise in Logical Order (page 165)

1. I'm the only person I know of who has ever fallen asleep while riding a bicycle in the snow.
2. When I was in college, I earned a little extra money by delivering *The New York Times* to people in the community.
3. The job was actually very pleasant in the spring and in the fall.

4. I dreaded winter, though, because there was always a lot of snow.

5. It's very hard to ride a bike in the snow, especially when the bike's basket is full of newspapers.

6. On Sundays, my customers complained if they didn't have their papers by 7 A.M.

7. Since I had 40 customers, I had to start my route at 5:30 A.M. on Sundays.

8. I stayed up till four o'clock one Sunday morning, studying for a big test that I was to take on Monday.

9. When the alarm clock screamed at 5 A.M., I couldn't believe it.

10. There was a blizzard raging outside; nevertheless, I loaded my bike basket with newspapers and started off.

11. I remember starting to coast down one slippery hill and then waking up in a snowdrift at the bottom.

12. I woke up just in time to see all of my newspapers being scattered over the mountains by the howling wind.

13. Now, 30 years later, whenever I settle down to read the Sunday *New York Times*, I still remember the day I fell asleep on my bike.

Irrelevant Information Exercise (page 167)

The irrelevant sentences are in bold type.

Contrary to popular belief, a snake's skin is velvety, not slimy. **When I was little, my favorite toy was a terrycloth snake that my mother made for me. There was a snake that lived under our barn, too,** and on hot summer days, he would sunbathe on a rock in the pasture. I named him "Norman," but he wouldn't come when I called him. Once, when I was in fifth grade, someone put a snake in my desk at school, and when I reached in to get my work, I touched him. His quick motion startled me, but after I calmed us both down, I stroked his skin and was surprised at how soft and smooth it was. I guess I had expected it to be damp and slimy, but it reminded me of the green velvet draperies in my grandmother's living room. If more people could actually touch snakes, perhaps they wouldn't automatically be repelled by them.

Additional Exercises for Recognizing Irrelevant Sentences in Paragraphs (page 168)

A.

3. I was born on a Monday.

4. Tuesdays aren't all that terrific, either.

7. Monday got its name from "Moon Day."

B.

3. The ancient Egyptians revered cats.

5. Catwoman was a nifty character in the *Batman* show.

7. My mother says that my aunt makes catty remarks.

8. My favorite song is "Kitten on the Keys."

Concluding Sentence Exercise (page 169)

2. All in all, people who don't want to gain weight should be very careful with butter, margarine, and salad dressings.

Index

223